THREE PSYCHOLOGIES

PERSPECTIVES FROM FREUD, SKINNER, AND ROGERS

Third Edition

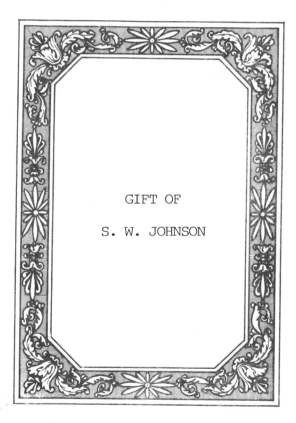

THREE PSYCHOLOGIES

PERSPECTIVES FROM FREUD, SKINNER, AND ROGERS

Third Edition

Robert D. Nye

STATE UNIVERSITY OF NEW YORK
COLLEGE AT NEW PALTZ

89-447

BROOKS/COLE PUBLISHING COMPANY
MONTEREY, CALIFORNIA

Consulting Editor: Lawrence S. Wrightsman, University of Kansas

Brooks/Cole Publishing Company
A Division of Wadsworth, Inc.

Printed in the United States of America

10   9   8   7   6   5   4   3   2

Library of Congress Cataloging-in-Publication Data

Nye, Robert D.
Three psychologies.

Includes bibliographies and index.
1. Freud, Sigmund, 1856–1939.   2. Skinner, B. F.
(Burrhus Frederic), 1904–   .   3. Rogers, Carl R.
(Carl Ransom), 1902–   .   4. Psychoanalysis.
5. Behaviorism (Psychology)   6. Humanistic psychology
I. Title.
BF698.N88   1986   150.19   86-9663

ISBN 0-534-06528-7

Sponsoring Editor: *Claire Verduin*
Editorial Assistant: *Linda Ruth Wright*
Production Editor: *Micky Lawler*
Interior and Cover Design: *Vernon T. Boes*
Cover and Interior Illustration: *Jerry Harston*
Art Coordinator: *Judith Macdonald*
Typesetting: *Graphic Typesetting Service, Los Angeles, California*
Printing and Binding: *R. R. Donnelley & Sons, Crawfordsville, Indiana*

Dedicated to my parents and others who have given me,
in various ways and at various times, ego-strengthening support,
positive reinforcement, and unconditional positive regard.

Preface

This book presents and compares, in a relatively simple and straight-forward way, a number of the major ideas of three men who have con-tributed greatly to contemporary psychological thought: Sigmund Freud, B. F. Skinner, and Carl Rogers. Beginning students who need basic information, advanced students who need review and updating, and lay readers who are curious about differing views of human behavior should find the book useful.

The main additions to this third edition are: a brief introductory chapter; recent interpretations and extensions of Freudian psychology (see the Commentary section of Chapter 2); Skinner's recent state-ments on education, aging, and social problems; and Rogers' current thoughts on education, world peace, and research procedures.

The introductory chapter gives an overview of each perspective and points out some of the differences among the theories. Chapters 2, 3, and 4 discuss the basic ideas of Freud, Skinner, and Rogers, in that order. I tried to present these ideas as convincingly as possible, holding back judgments and possible criticisms until later. The Commentaries at the ends of these chapters highlight certain important current aspects of each approach. Chapter 5 provides comparisons on specific issues, critical evaluations, and my own personal comments.

For the content of this book, my primary debt obviously is to Sig-mund Freud, B. F. Skinner, and Carl Rogers. Their contributions to psychology have provided a wealth of ideas to consider when attempting to explain human behavior.

A number of individuals aided in the preparation of the first edition, and their influence remains. My colleagues Kurt Haas, James Halpern,

David Morse, and Mark Sherman made many helpful comments, and Alan Stubbs, of the University of Maine, provided numerous suggestions regarding my explanations of operant conditioning. Judy Bufano did the typing in her usual patient, efficient, and good-humored way, and Wokie David assisted with this task. Also, I am thankful to Dean Scher for information on ego psychology and object-relations theory, which helped me to prepare the present edition.

The following reviewers contributed prerevision comments and suggestions: for the second edition, Glenn Carter of Austin Peay State University, Barbara Fulton of Western Michigan University, and Bill C. Henderson of the College of Alameda; for the third edition, Scott Fraser of the University of Southern California, Michael McGrath of the University of Nebraska at Omaha, and Charles Scontras of the University of Maine at Orono.

Several persons were involved actively in all editions. I am very grateful for the assistance and support of each of them: Lawrence Wrightsman, Consulting Editor for Brooks/Cole Publishing Company, consistently made thoughtful and constructive suggestions and kept me going with his optimistic outlook. Micky Lawler, Vice President of Production for Brooks/Cole, provided efficient editing and other production efforts, plus much consideration and encouragement. My wife, Eileen, supplied loving concern and helped in more ways than I can count.

I must also give special mention to Claire Verduin, Editor at Brooks/Cole. She has been a valued friend and adviser.

Robert D. Nye

Contents

1
INTRODUCTION
3

2
SIGMUND FREUD
AND
PSYCHOANALYSIS
9

3

B.F. SKINNER
AND
RADICAL BEHAVIORISM
49

4

CARL ROGERS
AND
HUMANISTIC PHENOMENOLGY
99

5

COMPARISONS, CONTRASTS, CRITICISMS, AND CONCLUDING COMMENTS
133

THREE PSYCHOLOGIES

PERSPECTIVES FROM FREUD, SKINNER, AND ROGERS

Third Edition

Introduction

The main ideas of Sigmund Freud, B. F. Skinner, and Carl Rogers have been with us for decades. These ideas, however, have not grown old (in recent writings, Skinner and Rogers have continued to expand their basic concepts). They still attract attention, cause debate, stimulate research, and gather criticism as well as praise. They form the bases for, or have influenced, many current attempts to understand and change human behavior, and they remain vital elements of present-day psychology—despite the rapid growth and expansion of the field in numerous directions.

Freud's psychoanalytic approach, Skinner's radical behaviorism, and Rogers' humanistic views actually constitute three different psychologies. They differ in the answers they provide to basic questions such as: What are the inherent qualities of human beings? What are the most important influences on personality development? What are the causes of problem behaviors, and how should these behaviors be treated? What should society do to maximize human achievements? What is the most effective way to study human behavior?

The fact that all three of these different perspectives currently have considerable vitality, and are not just significant historically, points out that psychologists have not achieved consensus on important basic issues. Psychology certainly is in good health if judged by the large number of persons entering the field, by the vast number of books and research articles being published, and by the public's interest in psychological matters. However, it is a field marked by numerous controversies. Psychologists often disagree. Reasons for this lack of agreement include the complexity of human behavior, the relatively short history of scientific psychology, and the problems caused by the fact that psychologists are humans who are trying to study humans (one problem is the difficulty of maintaining objectivity).

It could be argued that the controversies that exist among psychologists, though very disturbing when a definite answer is being sought, actually are additional signs of the field's good health. They show that psychologists often are unwilling to settle for a quick consensus and willing to take positions that they know will arouse criticism from at least some of their colleagues.

In producing controversy, psychoanalysis, behaviorism, and humanistic psychology play important roles; it would be difficult to find other viewpoints that have generated as much disagreement. Although many psychologists are eclectic, taking from each approach whatever seems useful, there also are firmly dedicated advocates of each of these perspectives, who try to defend and advance the particular approach that they have adopted. This makes for an interesting state of affairs, as well as some frustration.

It is challenging to have different theoretical explanations for behavior, with researchers of different persuasions attempting to validate these explanations. Discomfort may develop, however, among those (both inside and outside of psychology) who are looking for firm conclusions. Typically, I advise my students to try to develop tolerance for ambiguity, to learn different theoretical approaches well enough so that they can see clearly the similarities and differences among them, to realize that a theory can be partly right and partly wrong, and to understand that a theory can be useful in practical situations even if it does not provide final answers.

The differences among the psychologies of Freud, Skinner, and Rogers will become clear in the following chapters. Psychoanalysis, it will be seen, emphasizes unconscious personality dynamics. Freud concentrated on unraveling what he believed to be at the core of human personality: the hidden forces and conflicts that are buried deep within the psyche. He attempted to reach the unconscious by interpreting dreams (including his own) and by listening while his neurotic patients tried to verbalize their unrecognized, often socially forbidden, thoughts and longings. He believed strongly that sexual and aggressive drives are the root causes of our behavior and that early childhood is the critical period during which the individual's personality is formed through the interaction of these drives with the socialization process within the family.

Freud was skeptical about the possibilities for individual happiness, seeing a continuing conflict between primitive sexual and aggressive impulses and society's inhibition of these impulses. (He also was pessimistic about the future, believing that the destructive tendencies within us pose a serious threat to the continued survival of the human race.) While viewing happiness as an unrealistic goal, Freud saw his method of therapy (the psychoanalytic approach for which he is so famous) as a means for reducing neurotic anxiety and suffering by helping persons to better understand and cope with the powerful emotional tendencies within them.

In contrast to Freud, B. F. Skinner avoids going inside the person to explain behavior. Whereas Freud's ideas were influenced by his interactions with troubled patients, Skinner's basic assumptions were derived from studies of laboratory animals and were then extended to the human level. The behavioral psychology that Skinner developed is radical in its emphasis on external conditions as causes of behavior. While agreeing that our thoughts and feelings are important to us personally, he does not believe that these internal states determine what we do. Human behavior, he suggests, is governed mainly by its outcomes. During our lifetimes, various positive and negative consequences follow our behaviors, and these consequences are the most important influences shaping our "personalities" (that is, our actions and reactions in various situations).

Skinner argues that we too often ignore environmental effects and continually waste time and effort trying to understand and change what is going on inside (beliefs, emotions, motives, and so on). He is convinced that school, work, and personal behaviors could be vastly improved if positive consequences were provided systematically for productive, desirable activities. He warns that our society is in danger of being overwhelmed by its problems because of our failure to establish the external conditions that consistently strengthen and maintain beneficial behaviors.

Carl Rogers' humanistic psychology, the third approach to be considered, differs from psychoanalysis and radical behaviorism in significant ways. Rogers, for example, disagrees with Freud's view that humans are motivated primarily by sexual and aggressive drives. He asserts that fully functioning persons want to fulfill and enhance all their potentialities and that it is pessimistic and limiting to assume that sex and aggression are the most basic forces within us. With regard to Skinner's ideas, Rogers acknowledges that external conditions are important, but he insists that a person's feelings and self-concept play vital and undeniable roles in determining behavior.

Rogers developed his ideas while doing counseling and clinical work. He was profoundly affected by individuals who he believed were able to redirect their lives after achieving greater understanding of their real inner selves. He has been a consistently strong advocate of the power of the person to move toward self-enhancement once he or she has been set free to do so. The therapeutic approach that he founded, called client-centered or person-centered therapy, is designed to allow the individual to explore inner feelings and to make life choices based on greater self-awareness.

These brief comments on the psychologies of Freud, Skinner, and Rogers should make it clear that they provide alternative perspectives on human behavior. To be well informed about the current state of psychological thought requires familiarity with these perspectives. The following chapters give the basic information needed for understanding and evaluating the essential ingredients of each approach and for comparing them with one another. The references listed in the footnotes and at the ends of Chapters 2 through 4 will be useful for those who want further information.

Sigmund Freud
and
Psychoanalysis

■ BIOGRAPHICAL SKETCH OF FREUD ■

Sigmund Freud was born in Freiberg, Moravia (now in Czechoslovakia), on May 6, 1856. His father was a wool merchant, married for the second time. Five girls and two boys were born after Sigmund, and his father also had two grown-up sons from his previous marriage. Freud's mother was a lively and intelligent woman, and apparently she retained these qualities until her death at age 95.

The family moved to Vienna when Freud was 4 years old. Though their circumstances were quite limited, Freud's education was not hindered, and he did very well in school. He received his medical degree from the University of Vienna in 1881, after which he practiced medicine at Vienna's General Hospital and studied organic diseases of the nervous system. In 1886 he married Martha Bernays, to whom he had been engaged for four years. They had six children. The youngest, Anna, born in 1895, was to make significant contributions of her own to the field of psychoanalysis.

Also in 1886, Freud set up private practice, specializing in nervous diseases. Gradually his interests began to shift away from an emphasis on the physical aspects of the nervous system and toward the investigation of psychological causes of nervous disorders. This change in focus intensified during the following several years, resulting in full-time study of the psychological origins of neuroses. He continued this pursuit, while expanding his interests to include "normal" behaviors and social problems, until his death in London in 1939, at age 83. He

had been persuaded to leave his long-time home in Vienna the previous
year in order to escape Nazi persecution.

Among Freud's many important published works are *The Interpretation of Dreams* (1900), *The Psychopathology of Everyday Life* (1901),
Beyond the Pleasure Principle (1920), *The Ego and the Id* (1923), and
Civilization and Its Discontents (1930). Some of his best-known contributions were published when he was in his sixties and seventies.
His productivity remained at a high level throughout his life, and even
the pain and suffering of cancer of the jaw, for which he had 33 oper-
ations, did not deter his efforts to probe the human psyche.

Freud changed certain of his theoretical assumptions over the years.
Some of his earlier writings differ from the later versions of his theory
as presented, for example, in his *New Introductory Lectures on Psychoanalysis* (1933) and *An Outline of Psychoanalysis* (1940). The ideas
discussed in this chapter represent mainly the later stages of Freud's
thinking.

■ A DETERMINISTIC VIEW ■

Freud was a strict determinist who believed strongly that all behavior
is caused; actions, as well as thoughts and feelings, do not occur acci-
dentally or by chance. Making slips of the tongue, dreaming, hallucinating, forgetting, choosing, wishing, striving for success, repeating
certain behaviors again and again, refusing to admit mistakes, being
hostile toward others, writing novels, painting pictures, and on and
on—all these behaviors and all other behaviors were assumed to be
capable of explanation.

The Freudian view suggests that, if humans remain a mystery, it is
because of inadequacies in uncovering the driving forces within them
and the experiences that have influenced their behavior. Nevertheless,
these forces and influences *do* exist, and they *do* determine the person's functioning. It is the role of psychoanalysis to unravel the mystery
by seeking the sources of thoughts, feelings, and actions in hidden
drives and conflicts, and by investigating the ways in which the early
experiences of the person interact with basic human nature to create
the adult personality. The methods finally developed by Freud to examine the underlying causes of human behavior were preceded by his
interest in, and use of, hypnotic techniques.

■ HYPNOSIS ■

Early in his career, Freud came to believe that hypnosis could aid in
the discovery of the underlying reasons for psychological problems. In
1885 he left Vienna for a year to study in France with Jean Charcot,
who was using hypnosis in his work on hysteria. (This disorder bears
similarities to what is now called conversion reaction. The person "con-

verts" a psychological problem into a physical one; that is, because of emotional conflict, the person becomes blind, loses the use of a limb, or suffers some other physical disability. Even when it is explained to the person that there is no physiological damage or disease, the disability continues. There is a psychological, rather than an organic, reason for the disability.) Charcot found that the symptoms of hysteria could be produced in patients under hypnosis. These symptoms were the same as those that occurred spontaneously in the nonhypnotic state, and this discovery suggested that the causes of hysteria were psychological rather than physiological.

Freud returned to Vienna impressed with what he had seen, and eventually he began to work with Josef Breuer, a Viennese physician. Breuer had already used hypnosis to relieve the mental and physical symptoms of hysteria. His procedure involved having the hypnotized patient recall forgotten traumatic experiences while giving free expression to the accompanying emotion. He called this the *cathartic method.*

Freud's collaboration with Breuer was productive, and in 1895 they published a book, *Studies on Hysteria.* Their partnership was not to continue, however. Freud became more and more convinced that emotional disturbances had as their root some problem that was sexual in nature. Sex was a sensitive issue in the late 1800s, and Breuer apparently became uncomfortable with Freud's insistence on the importance of investigating sexual factors as the prime causes of emotional disorders. Freud was determined to surge forward with his line of thinking, and the two eventually parted company.

Another important development in Freud's approach occurred about this time. He was not satisfied with hypnosis as a technique. He found that some patients could not be hypnotized, that sometimes the hypnotic trance was not deep enough, and that relapses occurred. As an alternative that he considered better, he gradually developed the technique of *free association,* in which the patient relaxes (on the well-known analyst's couch) and says whatever comes into consciousness. This technique, along with *dream analysis,* is one of Freud's greatest contributions to the methods of psychoanalytic therapy. More will be said later about both of these methods.

■ SOURCES OF DATA ■

As Freud continued his treatment of patients, he formulated various ideas about basic human nature and about the development and structure of the human personality. These ideas were influenced not only by his contacts with patients but also by his reading of literature, by his consideration of events occurring in the world, and (very importantly) by his own self-analysis. In about 1897, Freud began to devote time to investigating his own inner thoughts and feelings, as well as his childhood experiences. He analyzed his own dreams and sometimes exchanged thoughts with his associates about the meaning of his and their dreams.

Psychoanalysis is both a theory of personality and a method of therapy. Freud tried to explain how we get the way we are (that is, how our personalities are formed), and he also formulated techniques to use in treating neuroses. He did not develop first one aspect of psychoanalysis and then the other; explanation and treatment developed hand in hand. As mentioned previously, early in his career Freud began to suspect that unconscious sexual conflicts were at the root of psychological problems. This was the start of the theory of psychoanalysis and provided Freud with a stepping-stone to further theoretical developments, which occurred as he continued to treat neurotic persons and to engage in self-analysis. There was an interplay between his theoretical formulations and his analytic observations, each influencing the other. We will now consider some of the most salient features of psychoanalysis as a theory of personality (often called psychoanalytic theory), and then we will briefly discuss psychoanalysis as a method of therapy.

UNCONSCIOUS, PRECONSCIOUS, AND CONSCIOUS: ■ "LAYERS" OF THE PERSONALITY ■

The psychoanalytic theory that Freud developed, and continued to modify over a period of nearly half a century, has as its backbone an emphasis on the unconscious aspects of personality. He certainly was not the first person in history to realize that humans are often unaware of their most basic drives, impulses, and internal conflicts. However, Freud's contribution is his *systematic study of the unconscious.* He made a prolonged and concentrated effort to tie together many, many bits and pieces of data from various sources in order to make sense out of the unconscious dynamics of the human personality.

In his relentless emphasis on, and pursuit of, the unconscious, Freud was not following the mainstreams of either turn-of-the-century medical practice or the relatively new field of psychology. Physicians were, by and large, not attempting to deal with psychological factors in disease. The tendency was to try to explain symptoms as resulting from some organic disorder or brain malfunction. Physical treatments were prescribed—drugs, tonics, hydrotherapy, electrotherapy. If these failed, it was generally assumed that the physical cause was unknown and that nothing much could be done.[1]

---

[1]Though it is commonly believed that Freud shocked and angered the medical community with his ideas, there are some conflicting opinions. For example, Frank J. Sulloway, in his book *Freud: Biologist of the Mind* (Basic Books, 1979), suggests that much of what Freud said was quite acceptable but that he chose to picture himself as a loner who was under attack.

The field of psychology at that time was taken up with the study of conscious states. For example, those psychologists who were following the approach called "structuralism" were attempting to break down conscious experiences (such as the perception of objects) into basic elements. Since they were interested in what we experience as we make contact with our environment, they placed the unconscious in a category that, by definition, is not subject to critical, scientific analysis.

Freud, on the other hand, viewed the unconscious as the part of the personality that *must* be studied. An iceberg analogy is sometimes used to illustrate the amount of importance given by Freud to the unconscious. Just as the major portion of an iceberg lies below the water's surface, the major portion of the human personality lies below the level of awareness; Freud believed that the really important causative factors involved in human behavior reside in this realm of the personality. Therefore, to understand human behavior, the unconscious *must* be revealed.

In Freud's *topography of the mind*, there are three levels of consciousness. The *unconscious* consists of all aspects of our personalities of which we are unaware. The *preconscious* consists of that which is not immediately at the level of awareness but is fairly accessible; many of our ideas and thoughts become available to us when we concentrate on them or attempt to bring them into awareness, but they are not constantly at the conscious level. The *conscious* consists of that which is within our immediate awareness. Actually, these three states of consciousness are not absolute categories but points on a continuum, varying from that which is clear and present to that about which we are completely unaware, hidden deep within the recesses of our personalities.

THE ID,
ITS INSTINCTS,
■ ## AND PSYCHIC ENERGY ■

In 1923 Freud published *The Ego and the Id*, which presented another way of looking at the personality: from a *structural model* consisting of the id, ego, and superego. The *id* is the most primitive part of the personality; it is the original system with which the newborn infant comes equipped. The ego begins to develop soon after birth, as the infant begins to interact with his or her environment. The *superego* represents the moral aspect of humans; its development occurs as the parents or other adults pass on society's values and standards to the child.

The id does not know "right" from "wrong," has no perspective on the possibilities and impossibilities of the real world, and has no inhibitions. It simply seeks gratification, operating according to the *plea-*

sure principle. Freud's concept of the id does seem to characterize the infant just after birth. The human at this stage of life has not yet experienced the difficulties of getting what it wants and has no moral convictions; thus, to think of the infant as "all id" is not unreasonable. After a while, the personality becomes elaborated as the ego and superego come into existence, being developed and molded by interactions between the person's inborn nature and his or her nurture (experiences with the social and physical world).

The id is where the human instincts reside.[2] Humans are born with *life instincts* (Eros) and the *death instinct.* The life instincts support and promote the survival of the individual and the species. Hunger, thirst, and sexual drives are aspects of the life instincts. Instincts have energy; in fact, the *psychic energy* of the instincts is what powers human activity. The energy of the life instincts is called *libido* (or *libidinal energy*). The term "libido" is often used synonymously with "sexual energy," since sex was the aspect of the life instincts with which Freud was most concerned.

The death instinct, sometimes expressed as the *death wish,* has a complicated origin. The theory of evolution suggests that the earliest, most primitive life forms emerged when certain chemical reactions brought inanimate matter to a living state. Freud assumed that these life forms were at first quite unstable; life was tenuous and reverted easily to its prior inanimate condition. Freud maintained that humans, though long removed in evolutionary history from these original forms of life, still carry within them a tendency toward death—that is, a tendency to return to the inanimate state. This tendency takes psychological form in the death wish, which may manifest itself directly, as in the case of suicide, or indirectly, as when people such as race-car drivers, mercenary soldiers, or other daredevil types engage in activities that involve high risks. Generally, however, the life instincts counteract the direct carrying out of the death wish. An important point must be stressed again: there is energy associated with both life and death instincts. Freud never gave a specific name to the energy of the death instinct, and it is generally called simply *destructive energy.*

All of the energy available to "run" the personality is provided by the instincts. This psychic energy is limited in quantity; that is, there is just so much available at any given time. As pointed out earlier, the seat of the instincts is the id. Therefore, the id initially contains the energy that eventually is "captured" by the other parts of the personality—the ego and the superego. The id is the original source from which the personality begins and grows.

---

[2]There is some confusion in various translations of Freud's works concerning the German word *Trieb.* Sometimes it is translated as *instinct* and at other times as *drive.*

Freud conceived of the human personality as an *energy system:* the personality at any given time is a distribution of energy among the id, ego, and superego. Since this distribution is ever-changing, it is extremely difficult to make *exact* predictions about human behavior. For example, sometimes we may be driven more strongly by our impulses (in the id) than at other times; sometimes we may be more realistic (as a result of ego functioning) than at other times; sometimes we may feel more morally bound (because of the influence of the superego) than at other times. However, even though there are changes in the distribution of energy, there is typically sufficient constancy to allow considerable, though not complete, accuracy in predicting a person's behavior.

■ SEX AND AGGRESSION ■

The two most important drives with which humans have to cope are the *sexual drive* and the *aggressive drive.* These are basic; they are part of human inheritance as aspects of the life and death instincts residing in the id. It is easy to see the logic of considering the sexual drive as related to the life instincts. However, it may be a bit more difficult to understand how aggressiveness toward other persons and objects is derived from the death instinct; after all, the death wish is originally aimed at oneself. A brief explanation is that self-destruction is usually prevented by the energy of the life instincts. Therefore, the typical person does not do away with himself or herself, despite the urgings of the death instinct.

The fact that the death wish is not often carried out directly in self-destruction (because of the counteracting influences of the life instincts) does not mean that the instinct is inactive. It has energy, and this destructive force cannot be completely bottled up within the person. In other words, destructive energy must be allowed some release. In fact, Freud believed that it is unhealthy to hold it back; illness can result if aggression is not vented in some way, either directly or indirectly. Release can be accomplished through displacement of the energy outward upon objects or persons in the environment. If this energy comes out in its raw form, direct destruction of property or other humans results. More commonly, however, because of social restrictions, some substitute for direct destructiveness is found. (This point will be discussed in more detail shortly.)

The idea of the death instinct was introduced in *Beyond the Pleasure Principle* (1920), and Freud later made clear his belief that a tendency toward violence and destructiveness is the natural human condition. He increasingly stressed this inborn death instinct, which tends to get turned outward in the form of an aggressive drive. Even when destructive energy gets diverted outward, however, some portion remains within. Eventually, of course, this portion of unreleased energy does win out and the individual dies; Freud suggested that perhaps death occurs when a person's libido (the energy of the life instincts) has been used up, allowing the destructive energy to have its way.

In *Civilization and Its Discontents* (1930), Freud emphasized the extreme conflict that exists between our basic pleasure-seeking nature ("pleasure" meaning the release of sexual and aggressive energy) and the existence of civilized societies. According to Freud, our innate propensities are to use one another for sexual and destructive satisfactions. In pursuit of these goals, we exploit, humiliate, torture, and kill one another. Civilization has not been successful in bringing peace among humans because we are, in our most basic nature, "savage beasts" who do not take naturally to the controls of our behavior that are exerted during the socialization process.

A primary result of human socialization is the incorporation of *guilt.* Guilt is an internal authority (a function of the superego) that is erected in the place of, and as a result of, the impositions of external authority. In plainer terms, we initially find that punishment and loss of love are forthcoming if we act on our basic, impulsive desires. This causes us to renounce our instinctive cravings, and we become afraid of our natural tendencies. The superego takes over the job of monitoring our behavior; "wrong" desires and wishes come to produce guilt feelings, and thus we control our own behavior.

Of course, it follows that civilization is in trouble whenever large amounts of instinctual energy are "bottled up" in individuals and denied release. This creates a very explosive situation, because it means that people are "boiling" below the surface; they are not releasing their libido and destructive energy and thus are in states of high tension. This might not be immediately apparent, since humans are capable of erecting *defense mechanisms* (discussed at length later in this chapter) against their inner, socially unacceptable impulses and drives. They may deny the existence of their sexual and aggressive tendencies; to admit their existence would be too anxiety provoking and would result in lowered self-esteem.

If society (represented initially by the parents and later by other influential persons in one's life) imposes strong, inhibitory demands on individuals and threatens to take away love and respect if these demands are not met, then it is likely that persons will come to reject, at the conscious level, desires that society deems wrong and immoral. These desires, since they are related to the basic instincts that Freud assumed we are born with, do not disappear because they are repressed. They still exist and may, if frustration levels are heightened, break through and result in antisocial behavior.

Another possibility that exists when instinctual energy is denied outlets is that our defense mechanisms will become more and more extreme. Because of the buildup of inner tensions, there is an increased necessity for us to protect ourselves from our basic nature. It is as though dark and evil forces (as defined by society) were operating below the level of consciousness—pushing, demanding, insisting on gratification. These forces can throw us into states of high anxiety; if they win out, love, respect, and self-esteem will be lost. The battle between these instinctual forces and the socialized aspect of humans is not fought out in the open; it rages mainly at the unconscious level, and we suffer from the effects of this internal conflict. Its rumblings disturb peace of mind and affect behavior; we are gripped by doubts and anxieties while only dimly recognizing the nature of the enemies at war within.

If civilization can provide socially acceptable avenues of release for libido and destructive energy, problems can be alleviated, though not completely solved. The process of channeling energy into alternative, substitute activities (rather than directly into sexual and destructive acts) is called *displacement.* If the displacement of instinctual energy results in socially desirable behavior, it is called *sublimation.* Civilizations progress because of sublimations; instinctual energy is used to write books, paint pictures, build bridges, do research, learn mathematical equations, and so on. It would seem, then, that a "good" civilization should make it possible for people to redirect their energies into various productive activities and that, the more this is done, the less the possibility that adverse outcomes will result from basic human propensities to engage in raw manipulation and misuse of others. Also, if sufficient sublimations occur, individuals are less likely to be tortured by internal tensions and anxiety. However, it should be made clear that Freud was not overly optimistic about these possibilities. He warned that the basic conflict between human instincts and civilization still remains. It must be remembered that sublimation is a substitute activity; as a substitute, it cannot completely satisfy the instinctive drives, and some tension will remain.

Freud believed that the *greatest* obstacle to a peaceful society is the destructive tendency in humans. Though problems are created by sexuality, since certain restrictions (and therefore some unhappiness) are necessary, acceptable avenues of release are easier to achieve than in the case of aggression. Also, a point that is sometimes overlooked is that the life instincts (Eros) were thought by Freud to include an urge toward union with others in the community, an urge that supports society (in *Civilization and Its Discontents,* he refers to this as an "altruistic" urge). Thus, while Eros is not completely opposed to smooth social functioning, the death instinct and its derivative, aggression, create much greater difficulties for society.

THE EGO AND ITS RELEASING
■   AND CONTROLLING FUNCTIONS   ■

In Freudian theory, the personality is considered to consist originally of the id. We are simply little pleasure-seekers when we begin life, and we do not know or consider reality. However, the realities of life soon begin to have an impact. For example, we are not fed every time hunger occurs, and therefore some discomfort and frustration are experienced. The response that the id makes to these tensions is called the *primary process.*

To understand the basis of the primary process, consider the example of the hungry infant who is eventually fed. During feeding, the infant sees, smells, touches, and tastes food. Repeated instances of this sequence result, in essence, in the storing of an image of food in his or her memory and in an association between food and hunger reduction. When hunger occurs in the future, the id engages in the *primary process* of attempting to achieve gratification (reduce internal tension) by forming an image of the object (food) that brought satisfaction.

Although the example of hunger was used, the primary process is not limited to the attempted reduction of this drive alone. Various images are formed to satisfy various drives. Dreams, wishful thinking, fantasies, and hallucinations are examples of the primary process in operation.

The primary process is active, but it cannot bring about a satisfactory release of the tensions produced by hunger, thirst, or sex drives. An image cannot be eaten, drunk, or erotically manipulated. To gain real gratification (that is, significant tension reduction), the individual must establish contact with the real world. This contact results in the formation of the second important system of the personality: the ego.

As the child interacts with his or her physical and social environment, the personality grows along a new dimension. Subjective functioning comes to be supplemented by increased reality-testing as things in the world are related to things in the mind; objects, persons, and activities that will satisfy the inner cravings of the instincts are sought. The ego develops through this interaction with reality. Whereas the id is completely subjective, the ego represents the aspect of the personality that strains toward objectivity; that is, it attempts to differentiate between what is desired and what is actually available. The *reality principle* guides the ego. In other words, more is considered than simply the impulse, the desire, the craving, the wanting. In a sense, the individual comes to ask "Is there something available to satisfy my longings, and is it attainable?" Realistic thinking, or the *secondary process,* is engaged in.

The ego attempts to reduce the tensions of the id, and it tries to do so by successfully dealing with the environment. Part of the "raw" psychic energy of the id's instincts becomes invested in the ego's functioning, which consists of finding ways of releasing more of the instinctual energy (thereby reducing tensions) and of holding the id's promptings in check until an adequate and appropriate means of release can be found. The ego can be thought of as the "control center" of the personality, either releasing or holding back the expression of basic instinctual drives, depending on internal and external circumstances. (However, it originally comes into being to serve the id, and this point should not be forgotten.)

The ego's investment of psychic energy in some object that will gratify the id is an example of a "cathexis." In a general sense, *cathexes* involve the attachment of energy to objects or the concentration of energy in certain processes. A loved person, for example, is a cathected love object. Psychic energy is invested in thoughts and processes involving that person. *Anticathexes,* on the other hand, involve the use of energy to restrain or inhibit. An example of an anticathexis is the ego's repression of an unacceptable impulse. (While the ego and the superego can be considered to have both cathexes and anticathexes, the id has only cathexes. It simply seeks gratification and has no restraints or inhibitions.)

The ego's functioning is affected by the demands and requirements imposed on the individual by parents and other influential persons—that is, the representatives of society. If parents and teachers are overly harsh and unyielding, allowing only very limited and highly specified outlets for instinctual energy, the child's ego is apt to be retarded in development. In effect, the child will not have the flexibility to develop a variety of effective ways of releasing energy; he or she will not be able to *sublimate* adequately. The result may be a buildup of tension, with resulting anxiety and inefficient functioning.

Freudian theory clearly suggests that a strong ego is the bulwark of the healthy personality. Freud proposed the criteria of being able *to love* and *to work* as indicative of good mental health. If environmental circumstances are not overly oppressive and limited, and if one's childhood includes a normal family life, persons should find it possible to work out compromises between their instincts and the everyday world in which they live. Love and work provide socially acceptable outlets (sublimations) for instinctual energy, and, if given some latitude and flexibility to investigate these possibilities, individuals should be able to develop reasonably satisfying adjustments to the real world while meeting, at least partially, the demands of basic human nature. If this can be accomplished, the person can be considered to have developed a strong ego, which functions as both a releaser and a controller of instinctual demands. Complete happiness is not the goal, since this is an unreasonable expectation from the Freudian point of view. Humans must accept, to some degree, the restrictions that civilization places on the uninhibited satisfaction of instinctual desires.

■   THE SUPEREGO AND ITS VALUES   ■

We have been discussing the id and ego and the origins of these two aspects of the personality. To complete Freud's picture of the structure of the human personality, we must also consider the development of the superego.

Parents typically are representatives of society. They have many values about the right and wrong ways to think, feel, and behave. These moral values are shared, more or less, by other adult members of their particular society. In the usual family situation, these values are passed on to the children: the result is that there is considerable continuity from generation to generation.

In Freudian theory, the *superego* represents the values and standards of the parents, incorporated into the individual's own personality. The superego develops as a result of the Oedipus complex (which will be discussed in detail shortly). The superego is a special agency of the ego, but it comes to constitute a third power within the personality, one that must be taken into account by the ego.

Most dramatically, we are aware of the superego's influence as a kind of internal judicial system that is referred to as the *conscience*, a term frequently used by Freud. The conscience often is a harsh and uncompromising internal judge of our thoughts and intentions, as well as our actions. It can observe, command, and threaten the ego with punishments, such as *guilt*. Although we sometimes can escape from or avoid the coercion and judgments of parents and others, the superego is an integral and ever-present aspect of our personalities. Also, it is capable of going beyond parents and other persons in its severity and unreasoning criticism.

In addition to its ability to punish, the superego can provide rewards. If the ego acts in harmony with the superego (for example, by resisting the temptation to do something "wrong"), a feeling of pride and heightened self-esteem may result. By behaving in accordance with the superego's expectations, the person can feel good about himself or herself. (Freud sometimes used the phrase *ego-ideal* to refer to the part of the superego that is the idealistic internal measure or standard of what the person should be.)

The superego strives for perfection and is seldom satisfied with less. It is, like the id, unrealistic. If it becomes too powerful (gains too much of the psychic energy that runs the personality), it will exert almost complete domination over the id and the ego, creating intense guilt as well as inhibiting the id's instincts and immobilizing the ego's attempts to achieve satisfaction in the real world. The number and intensity of do's and don'ts may be so great that the ego, figuratively, has nowhere to turn and shrinks into a corner of the personality, unresponsive to the cries for gratification emitted by the id and ineffective in the face of reality's demands.

Of course, for most of us, it is impossible to escape the learning of some set of values; indeed, such an escape would not be desirable. The psychopathic personality is a vivid illustration of what a person is like if he (or she) does not incorporate the fundamental values of society, and such a person could be considered as having a seriously under-developed superego. Psychopaths do not follow the rules and traditions of their society; neither do they consider the feelings and needs of others. Their behavior is impulsive and self-gratifying, without concern for consequences. Little or no anxiety or guilt is felt, even when serious harm is done to others.

A psychoanalytic explanation for the development of this type of personality would emphasize lack of parental love. In a typical home, parents do show love; that love makes it likely that children will identify with the parents and internalize their value systems (which usually reflect societal values). If there is no love, a child will not be afraid of losing it and therefore will be less likely to identify with the parents. (Other possible, nonpsychoanalytic, explanations for the development of psychopathic personalities can be given. Parents may be extremely deviant, fail to teach typical values, and serve as undesirable models for their children to imitate. Also, some cases of psychopathic behavior may be due to genetic or acquired brain damage, which can result in the inability to learn or retain moral values and standards.)

There are many in-between points on the morality continuum, with the extremely inhibited and restricted person at one end and the psychopath at the other. Somewhere along this continuum is the best position to point to when attempting to define the well-balanced personality. How to state precisely where that position lies is a difficult problem. Freud suggested that a strong ego is important for good functioning of the personality. Certainly from this it can be assumed that the superego must not rule or take over the personality. When we are functioning best as mature adults, the superego is a moral guide—but a guide whose directions can be considered realistically and accepted or denied on the basis of other feelings within us and also with consideration of the possibilities offered by the environment.

TOPOGRAPHY AND STRUCTURE: HOW THEY FIT TOGETHER

The id, ego, and superego constitute Freud's structural model of the personality. They represent his conceptualizations of different aspects of the total personality. It is important to remember, however, that they are simply that: concepts. They have no reality in themselves and should not be thought of as having actual existence. A personality cannot actually be cut apart and separated into id, ego, and superego, but for analytic purposes it is useful to distinguish among the various personality functions that these concepts suggest. A personality includes all of a person's feelings, thoughts, and actions, and it is ongoing and dynamic, not static. Freud's conceptualizations are meant to capture significant elements of the personality's structure as it undergoes a dynamic process of development during childhood and as it exists in a more firmly fixed state in adulthood.

Freud's topographical model of the personality (which preceded the structural model) consists of three layers of consciousness: the conscious, the preconscious, and the unconscious. Figure 2-1 shows how the structural model and the topographical model can be fitted together. (Here again, caution is in order. The drawing is meant for clarification, but drawings generally oversimplify abstract concepts and make them *too* concrete, giving a false impression that they actually exist and can be *directly* observed. This illustration is no exception. My hope is that clarification will occur without oversimplification.)

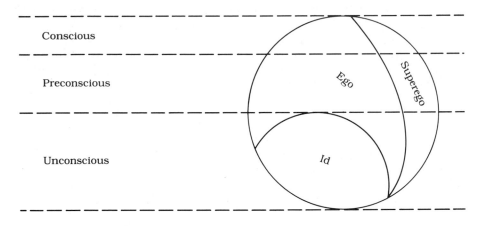

Figure 2-1. An integration of the structural
and topographical models of the personality

As the figure suggests, the id can be considered as that part of the personality that is totally unconscious. Our most primitive, basic, instinctive impulses (which are generally socially condemned and therefore not allowed into consciousness) reside here, and, although we may be completely unaware of their presence, they motivate our behavior and create internal conflicts. Along with these instinctive impulses, the id also contains other repressed material. When we feel, think, or do something that we have come to regard as unacceptable or threatening, or when we have an unpleasant experience, we tend to push it into the unconscious (a process that is itself carried out unconsciously, as will be discussed shortly); this material takes up residence in the id, joining with unconscious instinctual impulses to stir up trouble. The amount of stored-up material in the id differs, of course, from person to person. Because of different childhood experiences, some people are more aware and accepting than others of their total personalities; they are more in contact with their basic impulses and less likely to repress certain feelings, thoughts, actions, and experiences. One goal of psychoanalytic therapy is to "open up" the unconscious and to allow the person to come into contact with his or her deeper self—that is, the id.

It can be seen in Figure 2-1 that both the ego and the superego have unconscious, preconscious, and conscious aspects. Some ego functions (for example, realistic thinking and reality-testing) are conscious processes; older children and adults consciously construct plans of action, think about alternative ways of achieving goals, make choices, and so on. However, it must not be forgotten that the ego grows from the id. The instinctive demands of the id encourage contacts with reality, and the ego forms when some of the id's energy begins to be used for the pursuit of gratifications in the real world. The newly developing ego in the infant is not immediately distinguishable from the id; it becomes more clearly differentiated after significant attempts have been made to deal with the environment. Even after the ego has achieved some status of its own (exerting controls over instinctive impulses and giving consideration to reality), it still maintains, at its deeper levels, an interaction with the unconscious id. Also, it remains essentially in the service of the id. Thus there remains a part of the ego that extends through the preconscious and fades into the unconscious.

Freud pointed out another unconscious aspect of the ego: its repressing force. That which is unacceptable or unpleasant to the person may be cut off from consciousness—that is, repressed. To reduce anxiety and to protect self-esteem, the ego may act to remove discomforting impulses, thoughts, feelings, or memories. It does so in an unconscious operation; that which is repressed is unconscious, and that which does the repressing (the ego) does so unconsciously. A distinction can be made between *repression* and *suppression*. Repression is an ego-defense mechanism that occurs unconsciously. In suppression, we consciously decide to forget about something or avoid thinking about it.

The various contents and processes of the superego must also be considered as being at different levels of consciousness. We are quite aware of some of our values and consciously apply them. On the other hand, we sometimes experience guilt, feelings of inferiority, and self-doubts without being aware of the causes: unconscious workings of the superego. Many values are incorporated at a very early age and remain influential in affecting our feelings, thoughts, and actions, despite the fact that these values are not consciously realized in the present. Such values can make us "feel good" when we behave in accordance with them and can make us insecure, anxious, and guilty when we go against them.

Freud's concepts of unconscious, preconscious, and conscious layers of the personality seem to make sense intuitively. With a little introspection, most of us can realize that we are not always fully aware of the real reasons for all of our behaviors (that is, the "reasons" are at the unconscious level); we may at times feel vaguely troubled, guilty, or threatened without any apparent cause. At other times, we may not be immediately aware of why we are thinking, feeling, or behaving in particular ways, but with some effort we can come up with the reasons (which were at the preconscious level). Also, there are motives and various aspects of the environment of which we are quite aware (at the conscious level).

The structural concepts—id, ego, and superego—also can be applied easily to one's own personality. Most of us, at one time or another, experience urges to behave impulsively or have feelings or thoughts that startle us because they seem so primitively hostile or sexual (the workings of the id). We also try to figure out the best ways to relate to our physical and social surroundings in order to satisfy our needs (an ego function), and we are affected by moral considerations and make various value judgments (the superego's influence).

PSYCHOSEXUAL STAGES
OF DEVELOPMENT
■ AND THE OEDIPUS COMPLEX ■

Freud believed that the adult human personality has a certain amount of flexibility and can be changed to some degree; psychoanalytic therapy attempts, through a process that is often slow and painful, to bring about alterations in a person's feelings, thoughts, and behavior. However, even though the personality is not completely and permanently fixed by the time adulthood is reached, Freud believed that its basic structure and functioning *are* pretty well set during the first five or six years of life. He placed great importance on these early years and felt that much of what we are as adults is determined by early-childhood experiences.

Normal psychosexual development proceeds through a series of stages: the *oral stage* (roughly the first year of life), the *anal stage* (roughly the second year and part of the third year), the *phallic stage* (approximately the third through fifth years), a period of *latency* (from about age 6 to about age 12), and the *genital stage* (after puberty has been reached). However, Freud cautioned against thinking that the progression occurs in a clear-cut, definite manner. For example, there may be overlap in the pregenital stages (oral-anal-phallic), resulting in the coexistence of two stages at a given time.

In Freudian theory, the child's progression through these stages represents a complex interaction between nature and nurture. Human biology influences the basic pattern of development. However, many environmental factors (for example, parental laxity or strictness and relationships with siblings) determine the specific outcomes of the stages. In essence, then, physical maturation processes cause the primary focus of pleasure to shift from one area of the body to another (from mouth to anus to genital organs), and experiences during the developmental sequence affect the final outcomes in terms of individual personality differences. During socialization, the basic human needs and wants are gratified and frustrated in varying degrees in different individuals; because of our particular circumstances, each of us experiences somewhat different pleasures and satisfactions, as well as different pains and psychological conflicts.

The emphasis in psychoanalytic theory is on the first three stages—that is, the so-called pregenital stages. Each stage is named for the particular body zone that is the source of erotic pleasure during that phase of the child's development. Thus, during the oral stage, activity centers on the mouth, with sucking and biting occupying a good deal of the child's time. During the anal stage, the center of attention becomes the anus; the retention and expulsion of feces lead, respectively, to a postponement of pleasure and then to gratification. With the beginning of the phallic stage, the genital organs become important as the child engages in masturbatory activities and accompanying fantasies.

To pass through these stages successfully (with few resultant psychological conflicts or tensions) requires an optimal amount of gratification at each state—not too much, not too little. If too much gratification is received at a particular stage, there may be reluctance to move on; if too little gratification is received, frustration and anxiety might retard future development. For example, overly abundant oral satisfaction during the first year of life may cause a certain degree of *fixation* at this stage; as a result, personality development may be incomplete and as an adult the person may continue to be overly dependent on others and too optimistic that his or her needs will be met. On the other hand, if the infant is deprived during this period of life, his or her fixation may result in self-centered, demanding, and hostile attitudes as an adult.

"Fixation" means that some libidinal energy remains devoted to the concerns of an earlier psychosexual stage and is not shifted to later developmental stages. Therefore, full personality development through the most mature (genital) stage is inhibited; concerns continue to be, to some extent, immature. Fixations may be relatively minor or quite significant, depending on the circumstances during the particular stage and on the individual's reactions. All of us carry at least minor fixations into adulthood. Overeating, compulsive smoking, talking too much, drinking beyond moderation, nail biting—these are some examples of possible oral fixations. Traits such as stinginess, obstinacy, and over-concern about cleanliness and order may indicate fixations resulting from strict toilet training during the anal stage; the child's holding back of feces may have become exaggerated, and this characteristic may then have generalized to other behaviors. If a child is made to feel shame and guilt about masturbation and sexual fantasies during the phallic stage, insecurity and anxiety can develop; as an adult, the person might be overly aggressive, with tendencies to "show off" and brag as a cover-up for underlying, unresolved self-doubts and anxiety.

The most important event during the first five years of life occurs during the phallic stage: *the Oedipus complex.* Freud assumed this complex to be a natural aspect of childhood. It occurs in both sexes: boys develop a sexual attraction to the mother and want to possess her, displacing the father; girls desire to possess the father and displace the mother. (The female Oedipus complex is sometimes called the *Electra complex,* despite some resistance by Freud to the use of this term.)

As pointed out before, during the phallic stage the genital organs begin to take on considerable importance. Manipulation produces pleasure, and fantasies are associated with this activity. The child also begins to notice differences in the male and female sex organs by observing himself or herself, the father, the mother, brothers and sisters, and other persons. Since the dynamics are somewhat different for each sex, let us first consider the Oedipus complex in the boy.

One of the erotic fantasies of the boy has to do with possession of his mother. Along with this incestuous craving, the boy experiences resentment and jealousy of his father, and he may wish that this rival were out of the way. As the boy's imaginings intensify, an inner conflict begins to build. He continues to desire sole access to the mother, but he sees the father as a dominant and threatening figure who might seek vengeance if the boy's real feelings and thoughts were known. Therefore, *castration anxiety or castration fear* develops and becomes the main component of the male Oedipus complex. This particular type of anxiety or fear develops because the genital area is the most salient source of the boy's sexual attraction toward the mother. Other factors also play a role; for example, a father may warn his son not to "play with himself." Such warnings may be interpreted by the boy as threatening references to the feelings he has toward his mother, with an implication that something bad will happen to him if he doesn't behave himself.

So here we have a little boy undergoing great inner conflict resulting from a complicated mixture of conscious and unconscious longings, fears, and resentments. Of course, another complicating factor is that he still loves his father, even though he would like to get rid of him. How can all this be resolved? The normal resolution comes about through *identification* of the boy with his father. This means that he incorporates his father's values and standards within himself, thereby reducing his castration anxiety. (In simple terms, the father is unlikely to injure a son who is "Daddy's little boy"—that is, a replica of the father.) Identification with the father also serves social functions: cultural norms are passed on from one generation to the next, and the son learns the accepted masculine sex role.

Residues of sexual feelings for the mother and of hostility toward the father are likely to be repressed at this time. This repression may or may not create serious problems in the future, depending on the amount of material repressed and on the nature of events in the person's life. Events that are traumatic or highly stressful may precipitate a resurgence of repressed sexual or hostile feelings. An aid in bringing the Oedipus complex to a satisfactory conclusion, and in preventing the necessity of repressing highly charged sexual desires, is the transformation of incestuous impulses into acceptable, affectionate love for the mother. The dynamics of the Oedipus complex are extremely involved, however, and it is difficult to predict outcomes and future problems.

An extremely important aspect of the identification process is that the boy's superego undergoes its most significant growth. Freud stated that the superego is "the heir of the Oedipus complex." Because of the internalization of the father's standards of morality, a set of rules and regulations about proper and improper feelings, thoughts, and actions is established within the boy's personality and is an internal force that must then be reckoned with throughout life.

The resolution of the boy's Oedipus complex is not always positive. For example, resentment and hostility toward the father may continue and later generalize to all authority figures, or unusually intense castration anxiety may result in extreme passivity (a kind of "giving up" in the face of great frustration and fear). Homosexuality may develop if the father is weak and submissive and the mother is strong and dominant; identification with the mother instead of the father is a possibility in such cases.

Another factor that affects identification is the relative strengths of one's inherent masculine and feminine tendencies. Freud felt that everyone is constitutionally bisexual, by which he meant that each person's basic makeup includes same-sex and opposite-sex components. If a boy has certain family experiences (such as exposure to a weak father and a dominant mother) that combine with a relatively strong inherent feminine tendency, the likelihood increases that he will identify with his mother rather than his father.

Freud's explanation of the female Oedipus complex is even more involved than that for males and seems somewhat incomplete. However he did attempt to describe the critical events. For males, the threat of castration brings an end to the Oedipus complex; for females, the realization of the lack of a penis initiates the Oedipus complex. When the girl begins to notice differences in the genitals of males and females, she feels that she is missing something. As this feeling intensifies, it develops into *penis envy*. (Penis envy in the girl and castration anxiety in the boy are aspects of the total *castration complex*.)

Meanwhile, hostility develops toward her mother, whom she sees as the cause of her physical inadequacy. She rejects her mother and turns to the father for love. Of course, it is difficult for a little girl to simply give up her mother, so she tries to replace the essence of her mother within herself by *identification* with her. By trying to take her mother's place in relation to her father, and to share his penis, the girl becomes vulnerable to jealousy toward her mother. This increases the girl's already brewing resentment.

Freud believed that girls do not resolve the Oedipus complex in as conclusive a fashion as do boys, mainly because they are not motivated by the intense fear of castration that causes boys to move toward a more definite and complete resolution. He suggested that, for girls, castration could be considered as having already occurred; therefore it is not a present or future threat but rather a fact of life. Since girls do not bring the Oedipus complex to the same significant end as do boys, they also do not develop an equally strong superego. Freud believed that this lack of a well-developed superego accounts for feminine character traits such as emotionality, a lesser sense of justice, and a certain unwillingness to submit to the demands of life. (Feminists, and many other persons as well, have been very critical of these Freudian assumptions.)

To the extent that girls do resolve the Oedipus complex, identification with the mother and repression of the conflict are involved. If the feminine sex role is accepted, the wish for a penis may be replaced by the wish for a baby. Having a baby is assumed to be a substitute satisfaction that compensates somewhat for not having a penis. If a girl retains her initial wish for a penis—which, in essence, means that she wants to be a boy—she may grow up to have masculine traits and, in extreme cases, may be homosexual. Less dramatically, and more commonly, penis envy is likely to result in feelings of inferiority or shame because of "genital deficiency." (Again it must be pointed out that Freud's views on the female Oedipus complex, especially the notion of penis envy and its supposed effects, have been severely attacked as biased, male-chauvinist ideas.)

The primary cause of identification with the same-sex parent seems to be quite different in the Electra complex than it is in the male Oedipus complex. Whereas the girl's identification with her mother is an attempt to regain aspects of the lost love object, the boy's identification with his father serves to remove the fear of castration.

According to psychoanalytic theory, a reasonably adequate, positive resolution of the Oedipus complex is an important step in the growth of a healthy personality. Residues of psychological conflict involving unresolved sexual and aggressive feelings and thoughts toward parents can continue to create problems in adulthood. One goal of psychoanalytic therapy is to allow the patient to recognize and "work through" emotional conflicts and unrealistic parental attachments carried over from the time of the Oedipus complex.

Sometime during the fifth or sixth year of life, when the incestuous and aggressive impulses of the Oedipus complex have been partially repressed, partially converted into acceptable feelings, and partially resolved through the process of identification, the child enters the *latency period.* Sexual desires, hostile feelings, and fears are quieted to some degree. This period is often characterized by play with same-sex peers (which helps to strengthen sex roles through further identification) and feelings of affection and tenderness toward parents (although at the unconscious level there still remain some elements of sexual desire and aggression). This period of relative calm generally lasts until about age 12.

With the onset of puberty and adolescence, there is a reawakening of genital sexuality, but with a new emphasis. The pregenital stages are characterized by self-centered gratification-seeking; stimulation and manipulation of one's own body are the primary sources of satisfaction, and other persons are sought mainly to heighten these pleasures. The adolescent, however, begins to seek heterosexual relationships involving mutual gratifications. The earlier selfish tendencies begin to give way to a sense of caring and responsibility for the chosen sex partner. The socialization process continues, and, if conditions are normal, individuals enter the *genital stage* reasonably ready to take their place as mature, productive members of society, able to love and work in effective ways and accepting of themselves and the demands of the world in which they live. This assumes, of course, that they were able to weather the storms of earlier years without fixating seriously at some preceding stage or stages of development. Reaching the genital stage is not an all-or-nothing condition; functioning at this level is affected by the amount of libidinal energy available for appropriate concerns, which in turn depends on the extent of earlier fixations.

■ ANXIETY AND THE DEFENSE MECHANISMS OF THE EGO ■

The person who has successfully passed through the various stages of psychosexual development and is functioning as a mature, well-adjusted adult has an ego that is well developed. This individual's ego is strong and is able to handle reasonably effectively the demands of reality, of the id, and of the superego. Such persons have integrated the various aspects of the personality and function fairly smoothly in their environments. They are not beset with intense inner conflicts, do not feel racked by indecision and guilt, and do not feel overwhelmingly threatened or frustrated by everyday situations in their lives. However, even these persons are likely to suffer occasionally from temporary periods of anxiety. This anxiety is usually accepted as part of the human condition. On the other hand, some individuals suffer more intensely from anxiety; they are quite severely handicapped in dealing with themselves and with their social and physical environments. They have significantly lowered effectiveness in loving and working. Anxiety, which serves as a warning to the ego of impending danger, is greater if the ego is weak than if it is strong, since a strong ego can deal effectively with a greater variety of situations.

Freud suggested that there are three types of anxiety: *reality anxiety, neurotic anxiety,* and *moral anxiety.*

Reality anxiety results when there is some threat from the real world. The person is confronted with an external situation or condition that is perceived as dangerous. Anxiety may serve as a stimulus to take action to alleviate the threat; such an action then reduces the anxiety. If appropriate action is not taken, the anxiety may build up and incapacitate the person.

Neurotic anxiety results when the id's impulses threaten to break through and cause the person to do something that will be punished. The individual is afraid of losing control and getting into trouble. Of course, this fear is not likely to be fully conscious, and the person is apt to experience anxiety without being able to describe its cause. General feelings of apprehension and impending doom commonly occur.

Moral anxiety results from the superego's influences when the person thinks, feels, or does something that is in violation of incorporated values or moral standards. The superego is capable of producing guilt, shame, and feelings of inferiority when the person errs in his or her ways or even thinks about doing so. Moral anxiety involves a fear of punishment from one's own conscience.

It should be pointed out that reality, at least initially, also serves as a basis for neurotic and moral anxiety. The original learning of what actions will be punished and the incorporation of values and moral codes occur in relation to external reality as represented by one's parents and other influential persons.

As mentioned previously, the person with a strong ego is able to cope effectively with a variety of threatening environmental circumstances, has control over instinctual impulses while also providing constructive releases, and takes into consideration (without being immobilized) the values and standards that have been learned. To this person, anxiety serves as a useful signal that some demand—environmental, instinctual, or moral—exists and requires attention. Action is then taken, and anxiety is reduced before it reaches a high level.

For most people, however, the process doesn't always work this smoothly. Most of us need at least temporary defenses against anxiety in order to get through particularly trying experiences. We are not always able to be rational and to cope with ourselves and with reality in realistic ways. When we adopt unrealistic methods for dealing with the environment, with our impulses, or with our consciences, we are using *defense mechanisms.*

According to psychoanalytic theory, defense mechanisms are employed by the ego to protect the person from anxiety. Their use indicates a weakened ego—a state that may be minor and temporary or serious and prolonged. *Defense mechanisms involve falsifications of actual conditions and are assumed to operate unconsciously.* If they are used extensively for long periods, the person's functioning will be seriously affected; more and more extreme defenses may have to be erected as conditions worsen because realistic coping is avoided. In short, some use of defense mechanisms is probably common, but they have the potential to destroy effective functioning if they become typical responses to unpleasant internal or external realities.

Various writers (including Freud's daughter, Anna Freud) have attempted to enumerate the mechanisms to which Freud referred in his many writings. Among the mechanisms commonly described are repression, reaction formation, undoing, projection, rationalization, denial, identification, displacement (including sublimation), fixation, and regression.

Repression is the most basic, fundamental defense mechanism. The ego excludes from consciousness that which it cannot accept. Unpleasant or undesirable impulses, thoughts, feelings, or memories are either kept in, or pushed into, the unconscious because of their anxiety-producing potential. The ego must use energy (anticathexes) to block the material from rising to the conscious level.

Freud formulated his theory of repression in the early 1890s. He believed it to be a unique psychological discovery and gave it great importance as a primary and essential part of further theoretical developments. In his writings, he refers to repression as the "cornerstone" or "foundation-stone" of psychoanalysis.

In *reaction formation,* an anxiety-producing impulse, thought, or feeling is replaced in consciousness by its opposite. Hate may be replaced by love, resentment by affection, sexuality by "innocent" concern, and so on. The original impulse, thought, or feeling is not lost, however; it is simply hidden from consciousness by the opposite expression. Reaction formation can generally be detected because of the intensity with which the opposite emotion is expressed. For example, the defensive person may display so much love, affection, and concern for another that the recipient feels uneasy and "trapped."

Undoing represents an attempt by the ego to reconstruct previous actions so that they are less anxiety provoking. If a behavior or its consequences cannot be accepted, the weak ego may try to undo the act by wishing it away and making over the situation so that it is less unpleasant. Truth may be drastically distorted by the process of undoing, and the person may actually believe, at the conscious level, that he or she never behaved in an unacceptable way.

Projection is an attempt to get rid of one's own unacceptable characteristics by assigning them to others. It is as if the person were saying, "These cannot be my feelings, thoughts, or impulses, because they belong to him (or them)!" The person who is projecting may accuse innocent others of hating him, of wishing him harm, of wanting to "use" him, of being evil, of being hostile, and so on, when *he* (or *she*) is actually the one who is guilty of these emotions or thoughts.

Rationalization involves offering reasonable-sounding explanations for unreasonable, unacceptable behaviors; the irrational is made to appear rational to oneself or to others. If a person does something impulsive for which he (or she) is later sorry, he may not be able to accept the fact that he acted impulsively and may then construct a "good reason" for his behavior. Rationalization is also used to "explain" one's failure to achieve some goal. For example, saying "I wasn't really trying" can protect a person from the anxiety generated by being unsuccessful and losing self-esteem.

In *denial*, the ego is incapable of dealing directly with threatening facts in a present situation and therefore does not acknowledge the reality of this information. There is something in one's environment (external reality) that is too unpleasant to face; anxiety can be relieved, at least temporarily, by denying the existence of this aspect of reality. Denial may be accompanied by the substitution of a fantasy for reality. For example, someone may deny that a person whom he or she loved is dead and may keep the fantasy alive by saving the loved one's clothes or by leaving a room just as it was before the person died. In another situation, married persons may unconsciously reject various signs of a troubled marriage and continue to act as if their relationship were happy and satisfying.

Identification involves the introjection or incorporation of the qualities of another person. It can serve the purpose of removing the fear of a more powerful person, in which case it is referred to an "identification with the aggressor." For example, to resolve castration fear during the Oedipus complex, the boy typically identifies with his father. There is also "object-loss identification," which is an attempt to regain or restore a lost love object (person). This may be the basis for a little girl's identification with her rejected mother in resolving the Electra complex. Someone may also take on the characteristics of a loved one who has gone away or died, in an unconscious attempt to re-create in one's self that person's presence. As with other defense mechanisms, identification enables the person to alleviate threats and insecurities without directly facing them.

Displacement is the channeling of instinctual energy into an activity that is an alternative to the most direct and satisfying outlet, either because such an outlet is unavailable or because it is forbidden. Often we cannot directly vent our most basic sexual and aggressive drives. If *no* outlets were allowed, however, unbearable frustrations would result. Displacement permits a shifting from the most immediate form of gratification to some substitute form of gratification. Someone who cannot sexually possess or aggress against the *most* desired or *most* hated person often directs his or her attention toward some substitute person or uses energy in some other way. If a displacement results in some socially acceptable or beneficial activity, it is called *sublimation*. Freud suggested that the progress of civilization stems from sublimations, in which primitive, instinctive drives are redirected into constructive, productive activities.

Fixation and *regression* are related defense mechanisms. During psychosexual development, the person may *fixate* to greater or lesser extents at various stages. Too much frustration (perhaps because of too little gratification) or too much anxiety about the next step in development (perhaps because of overindulgence) may cause the child's ego to defend itself by "staying put," resulting in retarded personality growth. Later, when some unpleasant experience is encountered, the person is likely to be unable to cope effectively; as a defense against this uncomfortable situation, he or she may *regress*, or retreat to behaviors that characterized an earlier stage of development. Because of fixation, adequate ways of dealing with increased complexities and frustrations were not developed; now, when the person is faced with difficult realities, there is a tendency to return to the only ways of coping that he or she knows. An older child may continue to suck his thumb or "hide behind his mother's skirt" when faced with stressful circumstances. A young bride may run home to the security of her parents' home at the first sign of trouble in her marriage. A man in a new and difficult job may become "sick" and have to stay home and be cared for by his wife. A possible minor instance of regression (related to a minor fixation during the oral stage) is nail biting when under stress.

Most of the defense mechanisms have negative influences on human functioning. However, Freudian theory suggests that two of these mechanisms—identification and sublimation—have positive effects. Identification allows the values and standards of a society to be passed on from generation to generation, ensuring some consistency in expected norms for behavior. Sublimation involves activities that are beneficial to mankind and thereby promotes the development of civilization. (It sometimes is suggested by psychoanalysts that sublimation should not be considered a defense mechanism, since it doesn't lead to repression or psychopathology and isn't really defensive in the same sense as the other mechanisms.)

■ PSYCHOANALYSIS AS THERAPY ■

Anxiety and related neurotic symptoms cause individuals to seek help from psychotherapists. In Freudian theory, as we have discussed, there are three major sources of anxiety: threatening circumstances in the external environment (reality anxiety), the threatened breakthrough of repressed material in the id (neurotic anxiety), and the threat of guilt and other uncomfortable feelings generated by the superego (moral anxiety). Prolonged or intense anxiety indicates a weak ego, incapable of coping realistically with external problems and of managing internal conflicts. Unable to directly face and resolve external and internal anxiety-provoking circumstances, the weak ego brings defense mechanisms into use. Through distortion and falsification, and by self-deception, defense mechanisms afford some relief from anxiety, but they cannot be relied upon to provide a permanently peaceful state of mind. On the contrary, since they prevent awareness of real emotions, impulses, desires, and so on and hinder an accurate assessment of the external environment, they lead away from insight, understanding, reality-testing, and other possibly corrective, productive behaviors; thereby they cause the person to get into deeper and deeper trouble.

When anxiety-producing conditions continue or intensify, causing various symptoms such as fatigue, depression, guilt, headaches, impotency or frigidity, or feelings of inferiority and inadequacy, the person may decide or be advised to see a psychoanalyst. Not all psychoanalysts use exactly the same methods. Some are less traditional than others; that is, while maintaining an orientation that is basically Freudian, some analysts have made innovations on his techniques. The following brief discussion of psychoanalytic therapy focuses on the traditional methods developed by Freud.

As mentioned early in this chapter, Freud became attracted to the use of hypnosis in the 1880s. With Josef Breuer, he investigated its possibilities for bringing about cures for emotional disorders through catharsis, or emotional release, which was accomplished by the patient's talking out problems while in the hypnotic state. Freud's dissatisfaction with hypnosis grew as he found it difficult to hypnotize certain patients, to induce sufficiently deep hypnotic states, and to achieve permanent cures. He did, however, learn a great deal from his observations of hypnotized patients, and he came to the extremely significant conclusion that dynamic psychic forces operate unconsciously within the person to produce various neurotic symptoms.

To investigate these forces in a way that could be applied more generally, Freud developed the technique of *free association.* In order for this technique to be effective, patients must agree to follow the *fundamental rule.* That is, they must give up their efforts to maintain conscious and rational thought processes and say whatever comes to mind, no matter how trivial, disconnected, or embarrassing. Spontaneity of expression during free association is extremely important, and the fundamental rule is designed to ensure that patients will do their best to be spontaneous.

The analyst's couch, which is one of the most salient features in the stereotype of the psychoanalyst, was used by Freud to maximize conditions for the patient's deep reflections. Also, with the patient reclining on the couch, the analyst and patient do not have to face each other directly and continually; this makes for a more relaxed atmosphere and prevents unnecessary interferences with the analytic process (such as might result if the patient were to react to the analyst's facial expressions).

Another very important treatment technique developed by Freud is *dream analysis* or *dream interpretation.* Dreams have two levels of content. The *manifest content* is the conscious aspect of the dream and is what the patient relates when describing the dream. The *latent content* of the dream is the aspect that is most important in psychoanalysis; this is the hidden, unconscious meaning. Dreams, according to Freud, are expressions of unconscious wishes. That which reaches the conscious level is disguised and symbolic.

It would be too disturbing for the person if his or her unconscious sexual and aggressive impulses and desires were expressed directly at the conscious level; therefore a process called *dream work* operates. Dream work transforms the unconscious latent content into the more acceptable manifest content and involves several processes. *Condensation* can result in a number of latent elements being expressed as a single manifest element. *Displacement* can result in a trivial aspect of the latent dream being expressed in the manifest dream as something very important; the opposite is also possible—that is, an important latent element may seem trivial in the manifest dream. *Dramatization* is the process whereby unconscious elements are transformed into the visual images or pictures of the situations portrayed in dreams. In addition to these processes of dream work, *secondary revision* is also a common influence. This refers to the tendency to fill in gaps and make connections, so that the elements of the manifest dream frequently (but not always) seem to have continuity.

Freud considered manifest dreams to be filled with symbolism, mostly related to unconscious sexuality. For example, a penis may be represented in the manifest dream as a stick, a snake, a tool, or some other elongated object. A vagina may be symbolized as a box, an oven, a garden (to be "planted" with seeds), and so on. A woman might be represented by a house or a room, with the doorways being the body orifices. Sexual intercourse may be indicated by watering a lawn or climbing stairs. Hostility may be expressed by death or by an accident. These examples are relatively straightforward and obvious; in actual dreams the symbols are often much more complex and are interwoven in intricate ways, requiring great interpretive powers on the part of the analyst. (It must be pointed out that there is considerable disagreement, even among psychoanalysts, concerning the validity of Freud's views on dreams. Other ways of interpreting dreams have been offered, but the issue is too complex to discuss here.)

In Freudian theory, manifest dreams are *compromise formations.* That is, an unconscious wish is allowed some expression, but only in disguised form. The ego exerts censorship, even during sleep, preventing unacceptable unconscious material from surfacing in its actual forbidden form. When the ego fails to perform its censorship role adequately, the result is a nightmare (or, in psychoanalytic terms, an "anxiety dream"). In such cases the ego has failed to fulfill one of its important functions: to protect sleep by allowing unconscious tension to be partially reduced in a harmless way.

To digress for a moment, it must be pointed out that manifest dreams aren't the only compromise formations. Freud believed that neurotic symptoms also have this characteristic. That is, they too are disguised and distorted representations of unconscious, forbidden wishes. A clarifying example has been given by psychoanalyst Charles Brenner (see page 186 in his revised edition of *An Elementary Textbook of Psychoanalysis*). A woman's neurotic symptom of vomiting was assumed to be related to an unconscious wish to be impregnated by her father, a remnant of her unresolved Oedipus complex. Since the unacceptable wish could not be realized in consciousness, a compromise occurred. Vomiting, though a very troublesome symptom, provided some gratification of the repressed Oedipal desire—*it simulated morning sickness.* The anxiety that accompanied her vomiting resulted from the ego's unconscious guilt and fear concerning the forbidden wish.

The techniques of free association and dream analysis are used in combination in psychoanalytic therapy. Patients may be asked to freeassociate to some aspect of the manifest content of a dream in an attempt to have them reveal something about the latent content. The purpose of both of these techniques is to uncover unconscious material that is creating problems for the patient. An important step in the process of psychoanalytic treatment is to get things out into the open where they can be dealt with in the present. Repressed impulses, wishes, and conflicts must be brought to the conscious level.

The analyst attempts to take the role of an understanding and neutral listener as patients free-associate or relate their dreams or other experiences. Trust must be developed so that patients will feel that they can express their deepest feelings, no matter what these feelings may be. As unconscious material begins to be revealed, patients typically develop *resistances* to further revelations; that is, they may develop mental blocks, change the subject, sidetrack the discussion, try to postpone further therapy sessions, and so on. These resistances are brought into play for various reasons, many of them unconscious. An extremely unpleasant, hidden impulse or memory may be on the verge of becoming realized at the conscious level; the resulting anxiety may overwhelm the ego, which then erects a block against the offensive material. In such a case, the person is not yet ready to accept this aspect of himself or herself.

Various types of resistance are common during the analytic process. In essence, they represent forces within the person that oppose the process of positive change. In addition to the ego's attempts to prevent disturbing material from surfacing, resistance can occur for the following reasons: (1) Resentment and frustration may result when the analyst does not meet the patient's unrealistic expectations, and the patient may then become less cooperative. (2) Neurotic symptoms such as intense anxiety, persistent headaches, chronic fatigue, and depression may serve useful purposes for the person, despite the fact that they also cause much discomfort. They can provide excuses for avoiding responsibilities, and they may attract attention and sympathy from others; therefore they are not given up easily. These benefits are referred to as *secondary gains*. (3) The self-destructive urge that Freud said is basic to human nature may operate to maintain harmful behaviors and states of mind. (4) The superego can exert influence, sometimes resulting in a deep-seated feeling in the patient that he or she should continue to suffer for various transgressions. Though this list does not exhaust the possible sources of resistance, it does show that there are a number of forces acting against the patient's improvement. Resistances can occur with varying degrees of recognition by the patient, from the conscious to the unconscious level.

The analyst must remove resistances if therapy is to proceed in a beneficial way, so that deeper and deeper levels of the unconscious can be exposed. A technique that is used is *interpretation:* the analyst tries to explain to patients the irrational qualities of their resistances. Timing is important in interpretation. Done too soon, it may result in increased resistance, may give patients explanations that they accept too readily (so that they think they are "cured"), or may be accepted solely on an intellectual, rather than an emotional, level. Patients must be persuaded to give up their resistances if they are to gain insight into the underlying dynamics of their neurotic symptoms.

Psychoanalytic treatment involves, in a sense, a reliving of one's past. Childhood feelings and conflicts emerge from the deep recesses of the unconscious; there is an emotional regression. As patients once again experience these old emotions, they tend to attach them to the analyst. This process is called *transference.* Patients may, at different times, see the analyst as a punitive father, as a demanding mother, as a seductive lover, and so on. These emotional attachments must be "worked through" if cure is to be the eventual outcome of the analysis. In "working through" transferences, patients have the chance to re-experience earlier relationships and to bring them to a more satisfactory resolution.

Transference does not usually operate in an obvious and direct way; it is more likely that the emotions of the patient will manifest themselves toward the analyst in subtle ways. Here again, the analyst must be sensitive to these subtleties and must provide interpretations only at the proper time. Also, he or she must guard against *countertransference,* which is an emotional reaction to the patient. The analyst must be able to remain objective in the face of adulation, praise, criticism, anger, and other emotional expressions by the patient. A common requirement during psychoanalytic training is that future analysts undergo psychoanalysis themselves. A personal analysis is intended to reduce the possibility that psychoanalysts will bring their own unresolved conflicts into their professional work. They must retain sufficient distance from patients to allow careful, accurate, and penetrating interpretations of behaviors that are irrational and self-defeating.

Here, in brief, is a summary of the basic psychoanalytic techniques and processes we have discussed: *Free association* and *dream analysis* are used to tap the patient's unconscious. When the patient offers *resistances* to the uncovering of unpleasant unconscious material or to the responsibilities involved in being cured, the analyst must supply *interpretations* of these irrational behaviors. The patient will engage in *transferences,* attaching past emotional feelings to the analyst in the present situation. These transferences have to be "worked through" with the assistance of the analyst, who must avoid *countertransferences.* Obviously, more is required for cure than simple insight on the part of the patient. He or she has to deal with the emotional components of unconscious material, which are manifested in resistances and transferences.

Psychoanalytic treatment is generally a long and arduous process, often requiring several sessions per week for years. The patient undergoes an educational experience of a deeply emotional nature. The goals are self-awareness, honesty, better control over impulses, more effective interpersonal relations, more realistic assessments of potentialities, and the ability to accept that which cannot be changed. Happiness as an absolute state is not the goal; according to Freud, the human condition is not one that allows this achievement. We must learn to accept certain weaknesses and limitations in ourselves and in others. The person with a sufficiently strong ego can do this, and psychoanalytic treatment is designed to strengthen the ego.

■ **COMMENTARY** ■

Interesting questions continue to be raised about our understanding of psychoanalysis. Bruno Bettelheim, the well-known psychoanalyst and child psychologist, claims that English translations of Freud's writings have distorted certain basic concepts and have given a misleading impression of Freud's message.[3] He gives many examples to support his argument that Freud's thinking has been misrepresented by translators. For instance, where Freud used the German word "Ich," translators have used the Latin equivalent "ego" instead of the more accurate, simple, and personal "I." Bettelheim suggests that "ego" and other translations, such as id, superego, and cathexis, make psychoanalysis seem coldly technical, impersonal, and esoteric. These terms do not arouse the personal and emotional associations that he believes are vitally important for a proper understanding of Freudian psychology.

The word "psychoanalysis" is itself misunderstood, according to Bettelheim. He suggests that Freud intended to emphasize the need to investigate one's own soul (psyche), meaning one's deepest human emotions, in order to live a fuller, richer life through self-discovery. In English usage, the emphasis often is on the latter part of the word (analysis), conveying an overly scientific and depersonalized meaning and implying that the behavior of others, rather than one's own, needs analyzing. In Bettelheim's view, Freud's concerns were deeply humanistic. That is, he wanted to pave the way toward a more gratifying life of work and love by encouraging individuals to recognize their own unconscious drives, and he attempted to appeal to our common humanity without being highly theoretical or formally scientific.

It is difficult to know whether or not Bettelheim has overstated his case. Do those of us who read Freud in English translations really misunderstand his message? Was it more personal, simple, and humanistic than commonly is thought? Bettelheim is not the first person to point out possible problems in translations of Freud's writings, and it would seem wise to avoid being overly confident about our precise understanding of every aspect of psychoanalysis as Freud intended it to be understood. There are difficulties in conveying exact meanings even in one's own language, so certainly there are likely to be some problems in translations to a different language.

Addressing a very different issue with regard to our understanding of psychoanalysis, Jeffrey Masson, former projects director of the Sig-

[3]Bruno Bettelheim, *Freud and Man's Soul* (New York: Knopf, 1982).

mund Freud Archives, has started a heated controversy.[4] He paints a much less flattering picture of Freud than does Bettelheim. Masson asserts that Freud, for complex personal reasons, failed to persist in his original view that his patients generally were the victims of childhood sexual abuse. Instead, Freud promoted the idea that memories of such events involve fantasies related to infantile sexuality and the Oedipus complex. In other words, Masson accuses Freud of unjustifiably shifting the causation of neuroses from external trauma to internal conflict.

Freud, in 1896, stated his belief that his patients (mainly his women patients) were suffering the effects of actual childhood sexual traumas, such as incest and rape. This came to be called the "seduction theory." During the following years, Freud wavered in his position and finally settled on the idea that such experiences usually are not real but instead are based on fantasy. Masson contends that Freud had no sound basis for giving up his seduction theory; it seems that he lacked the courage necessary to hold fast to the unpopular and distasteful view that children were being made severely neurotic because of sexual abuse by their parents or other adults.

Among the reasons Freud gave for changing his belief were his growing doubts that sexual acts against children could be so widespread and his view that patients were unable to distinguish clearly between fact and fiction emerging from the unconscious (and therefore were not likely to report accurately on events during early childhood). Masson suggests, however, that the real explanations for Freud's turnabout more likely were personal, including his reaction to ostracism by colleagues, his reluctance to pursue the idea that fathers (perhaps including his own) were guilty of sexually abusing their children (primarily their daughters), and his desire to protect an intimate friend, physician Wilhelm Fliess.

On Freud's recommendation, Fliess had performed a nasal operation on one of Freud's female patients, after which she experienced severe bleeding from the nose. By suggesting that the patient's bleeding was the result of her wish to be cared for, rather than the result of bungled surgery, Freud removed the blame from Fliess. (How severe bleeding could be caused by a wish was left unexplained.) Masson believes that this case of downplaying an external cause (a surgical error), and substituting an internal cause (the patient's wish to be cared for), was an important step on Freud's path to the rejection of the seduction theory (which focused on external causes).

[4]Jeffrey M. Masson, *The Assault on Truth: Freud's Suppression of the Seduction Theory* (New York: Farrar, Straus and Giroux, 1984). A briefer account can be found in Masson's article "Freud and Seduction Theory," *The Atlantic Monthly*, February 1984, pp. 33–60.

Of what consequence was Freud's rejection of the seduction theory? Masson argues that shifting the cause of neuroses from external traumatic events to an emphasis on internal fantasies (notably, sexual and aggressive fantasies that supposedly occur during the Oedipal period) does a serious disservice to patients. He suggests that children are abused sexually much more commonly than is generally acknowledged and that such abuse too often is ignored by analysts who convince their patients that memories of such experiences are fantasies. The whole analytic process thereby becomes distorted. If the patient is to become "healthy," he or she must accept the view that internal fantasies, impulses, and conflicts are at the heart of the neurosis, and must deny the possibility of actual childhood experiences of sexual abuse. This is likely to cause continuing guilt, uncertainty, dependency, and lack of an adequate sense of self.

What is the truth regarding Masson's allegations? Did Freud abandon the seduction theory for personal, rather than objective, reasons? And—more importantly—are patients in analysis often the victims of actual sexual abuse who are being treated inappropriately by their analysts? Masson's opinions, as he himself has indicated, are the result of his interpretations of documents (including previously unexamined letters from Freud to his close friend, Wilhelm Fliess) that others might interpret differently. It is impossible to know with complete certainty what Freud's motives were; they can only be assumed. Also, it can't be known with absolute certainty whether or not actual events of childhood sexual abuse are as common as Masson suggests, although there are other recent authors who agree with his assessment.

There has been considerable hostility in the psychoanalytic community toward Masson and his ideas. Understandably, those who have long accepted Freud's revised view, emphasizing childhood sexual fantasies, are reluctant to consider that this revision may have been unjustified. In my own opinion, however, Masson's assertions deserve careful consideration, especially by those engaged in analytic therapy who may be ignoring the possibility that their patients are suffering from the effects of actual sexual abuse. (In fairness to Freud it should be mentioned that, even after he revised the seduction theory, he did not deny the possibility that actual sexual offenses against children sometimes do occur.)

Bettelheim and Masson are just two of the many scholars who have interpreted Freud's work. Among these interpreters are both strong supporters and harsh critics. Considering the extent and variety of his writings, there is little wonder that different opinions exist. Undoubtedly, there will continue to be controversies as further studies are done.

Moving on from the topic of Freud's interpreters, let's consider briefly some current aspects of psychoanalysis. Modern psychoanalysts are a mixed group. Besides the orthodox believers who stay close to Freud's basic formulations and analytic techniques, there are those who fall along a continuum extending to theoretical views and therapeutic procedures that are considerably different from his. Some differences are based on major issues, such as the extent to which cultural, versus instinctual, forces should be considered as determinants of personality development. Others are based on relatively minor points, such as whether the analyst should sit facing a seated patient, instead of following Freud's example of sitting behind a reclining patient.

Psychoanalysis has its largest number of adherents in the United States. They are found mainly in urban areas such as Boston, New York, Chicago, and Los Angeles. The rise of psychoanalysis in this country was influenced by World War II, when a number of European analysts moved here.

The training of psychoanalysts is an issue about which there has been heated controversy. Freud himself suggested (despite the fact that he had a medical degree) that medical training is *not* necessary before undergoing the essential preparation, which involves extensive study of relevant literature and analytic techniques, an intensive personal analysis, and careful supervised treatment of patients. In the United States, however, there has been a strong tradition of the M.D. degree being a prerequisite for becoming a psychoanalyst. "Lay analysts" (that is, nonmedical analysts) have had trouble gaining full acceptance in the psychoanalytic community. The prestigious American Psychoanalytic Association (which has about 2800 members) and its affiliated training institutes have been restricted primarily to those in the medical profession. Though several psychoanalytic institutes, including the William Alanson White Institute in New York City and the Los Angeles Institute for Psychoanalytic Studies, do accept psychologists, these are exceptions. Psychologists' attempts to gain equity with physicians in access to psychoanalytic training include a recent antitrust suit against the American Psychoanalytic Association.[5]

There have been several theoretical changes in psychoanalysis since Freud's death, some of which are more widely accepted than others. One of the major changes has been a growing emphasis by a number of analysts on autonomous ego functions. This emphasis is reflected in the phrase "ego psychology." A prime mover in this development was Heinz Hartmann.[6] Whereas Freud saw the ego as essentially subservient to the demands of the id (though the ego could gain some amount of control), Hartmann and his colleagues give greater autonomy to the

---

[5]See "Analysts Sued for Barring Non-MDs," *APA Monitor*, May 1985, p. 2. The *Monitor* is the monthly newspaper of the American Psychological Association.

[6]One of his works is *Essays on Ego Psychology* (New York: International Universities Press, 1964).

ego. In fact, they consider the ego, as well as the id, as having origins in basic human inheritance. In their view, the ego has its own developmental course and operates on neutralized energy, which makes possible an interest in objects and activities that are not necessarily related to underlying sexual or aggressive drives. (Though Freud at times also seemed to be suggesting that such interests are possible, his dominant theme is different: objects and activities are "interesting" to the person primarily because they are related, directly or indirectly, to the basic personality components of sex and aggression.)

If Freud had lived longer, perhaps he would have moved in the direction of emphasizing autonomous ego functioning. In 1937 (in a paper titled "Analysis Terminable and Interminable") he suggested that the ego's development and characteristics may be determined by hereditary factors that are present prior to its existence. This implies a greater independence of the ego from the id than generally is assumed in Freudian theory. Though Freud himself did not have the time to further pursue this line of thought, Hartmann and others have advanced the assumption of ego autonomy.

It's likely that the increased attention given to an independent ego has resulted partly from a change in the types of patients that psychoanalysts are treating. The world is different from what it was around the turn of the century, when Freud and other psychoanalytic pioneers were developing ideas from their clinical experiences. In recent years, patients tend more often to be troubled by the problems of an increasingly complex society (vague anxieties, insecurities, and dissatisfactions) and are seeking ways to find meaning and values in work, family, and social roles. Since the ego is the part of the personality that must deal with the external world in some rational, decision-making way, it seems natural that more emphasis should be given to it. Perhaps for the contemporary patient it is important to focus more attention on conscious thought processes and coping mechanisms; he or she is probably less likely to be plagued by unconscious guilt and repressed sexuality than by the uncertainties and rootlessness of modern society that require the ego to grapple with existential problems.

A person who has been very influential in bringing a strong social flavor to contemporary psychoanalysis, while also emphasizing the ego's functions, is Erik H. Erikson. Trained in Vienna, he worked with Freud's daughter, Anna (also a psychoanalyst), and in 1933 came to the United States, where he held various academic and research positions and practiced psychoanalysis. His most important book is generally considered to be *Childhood and Society*, first published in 1950.

Erikson postulates eight *psychosocial* stages of development, which represent an expansion and elaboration, in primarily social terms, of Freud's *psychosexual* stages. Freud was concerned mainly with personality development based on the working out of emerging sexual needs, and his last stage (the genital stage) did not detail the adult years. Erikson's emphasis is on the social influences that occur during various developmental stages, and his last three stages cover the adult years from young adulthood to old age. He points out various social experiences, with their accompanying expectations and demands, that occur during the person's life span.

The human ego, according to Erikson, has the potential to deal creatively with these experiences and to produce such positive outcomes as competency, a sense of purpose, the ability to love, and wisdom in old age. He also believes that failure at one stage does not necessarily doom one to life-long failure; the person, sometimes with the help of a psychoanalyst, often is capable of recovering. In Erikson's opinion, the ego has much potential strength, and he chooses to concentrate more on this part of the personality and its conscious functioning than on the irrational, unconscious aspects of the mind.

Another development that has its roots in Freudian psychology, and is tied closely to ego psychology, is the currently popular "object-relations theory."[7] While agreeing with Freud's assumption that early-childhood experiences powerfully affect the adult personality, this newer approach focuses greater attention on the pre-Oedipal period of development. What is stressed is the significance of the internal images that come to represent external objects (for example, the infant internalizes the object "mother"). Object-relations theory suggests that the conscious and unconscious meanings associated with these internalized images determine, in a complex way, the patterns of our relationships with others.

With the changes made by Hartmann, Erikson, and many others in certain assumptions and emphases of Freudian theory, what is the present status of psychoanalysis? This isn't an easy question to answer. Certainly it can be said, as mentioned earlier, that the psychoanalysts of today represent a wide range of views. Despite the criticisms of traditional analysts, who claim that psychoanalysis is being watered down by those who deviate from Freud's basic teachings, changes seem inevitable. These changes may prevent psychoanalysis, as a formal discipline, from becoming simply a relic of times past. On the other hand, they may eventually dilute it to the point where its essence is lost.

---

[7]For example, see Lillian B. Rubin's *Intimate Strangers: Men and Women Together* (New York: Harper & Row, 1983). For a brief historical perspective, see Anita M. Mendez's and Harold J. Fine's "A Short History of the British School of Object Relations and Ego Psychology," *Bulletin of the Menninger Clinic,* Vol. 40, No. 4, 1976, pp. 357–382. An interesting, though fairly complex, book is Jay R. Greenberg's and Stephen A. Mitchell's *Object Relations in Psychoanalytic Theory* (Cambridge, Mass.: Harvard University Press, 1983).

There are some who believe that psychoanalysis already is dead and is simply waiting for burial. They see attempts to redefine its emphases, or to maintain its vitality, as revival efforts that have come too late with too little sustenance.[8] In contrast to these critics are those who see psychoanalysis, especially in its updated forms, as being in good health with a promising future.[9]

Whether psychoanalysis sinks or continues to swim as a formal approach and school of thought, its impact on our society has been assured, and that impact is unlikely to disappear for a long time. It has numerous manifestations: (1) Research projects continue to test aspects of Freudian psychology,[10] and new books on psychoanalysis continue to appear. (2) Many mental-health practitioners—including psychotherapists, counselors, and social workers—while not trained formally as psychoanalysts, have incorporated elements of Freudian thought and technique into their approaches to the problems of their patients. (3) In many college courses in the social sciences and humanities, Freud's ideas are discussed and considered for their historical interest and possible contemporary relevance. (4) There are scholars who remain interested in the study of Freudian theory as a social philosophy, apart from its clinical implications and applications. This approach was started by Freud himself; especially in his later writings, his attention turned increasingly toward the relationships and tensions between individuals and society. (5) Much literature, both classic and popular, shows strong Freudian themes, such as the effects of early-childhood traumas, unconscious conflicts, and repressed desires. (6) Our everyday language is sprinkled with Freudian terms. People frequently talk about their own or others' repressions, defenses, hidden wishes, ego strength, and so on, often without knowing that these concepts are common because of Freud's influence on our culture.

Freud's ideas are with us in various forms. Whether or not this is desirable is a question whose answer depends on one's assessment of the validity and usefulness of his assumptions and suggestions. Arguments concerning this issue abound.

---

[8]For example, see Carl Rogers' comments in Richard I. Evans' *Carl Rogers: The Man and His Ideas* (New York: Dutton, 1975), pp. 88–90.

[9]For example, see Calvin S. Hall's and Gardner Lindzey's comments in the third edition of their textbook *Theories of Personality* (New York: Wiley, 1978), pp. 75–87.

[10]Some of this work is described by Lloyd H. Silverman in "Psychoanalytic Theory: 'The Reports of My Death Are Greatly Exaggerated,' " *American Psychologist*, Vol. 31, No. 9, September 1976, pp. 621–637. The research of Silverman and his colleagues also is discussed by Virginia Adams in "Mommy and I are one: Beaming messages to inner space," *Psychology Today*, May 1982, pp. 24–36, and by Silverman and Joel Weinberger in "Mommy and I are one: Implications for psychotherapy," *American Psychologist*, Vol. 40, No. 12, December 1985, pp. 1296–1308.

■ REFERENCES FOR CHAPTER 2 ■

Primary Sources (Freud's Own Writings)

Translations of Freud's writings are found in many forms put out by various publishers. Hogarth Press of London has published a complete Standard Edition of his works, consisting of 24 volumes.

The following are paperbound editions to which I referred while writing this book. They can be found relatively easily, since many bookstores stock them. The interested reader should be able to obtain them without difficulty.

1. *The Interpretation of Dreams.* New York: Avon Books.
2. *Beyond the Pleasure Principle.* New York: Bantam Books.

All of the following are published by W. W. Norton and Company, New York:

3. *An Autobiographical Study*
4. *Civilization and Its Discontents*
5. *The Ego and the Id*
6. *New Introductory Lectures on Psychoanalysis*
7. *On Dreams*
8. *On the History of the Psycho-Analytic Movement*
9. *An Outline of Psychoanalysis*
10. *The Problem of Anxiety*

The following is a clothbound volume:

11. *The Basic Writings of Sigmund Freud.* New York: Random House, 1938. (Introduction by A. A. Brill.)

Secondary Sources

1. Brenner, Charles. *An Elementary Textbook of Psychoanalysis.* (Rev. ed.) New York: International Universities Press, 1973. (Also in paperbound edition by Anchor Books.)
2. Freud, Anna. *The Ego and the Mechanisms of Defense.* (Rev. ed.) New York: International Universities Press, 1966.
3. Hall, Calvin S. *A Primer of Freudian Psychology.* Cleveland: World, 1954. (Also in Mentor paperbound edition by The New American Library.)
4. Hall, Calvin S., & Lindzey, Gardner. *Theories of Personality.* (3rd ed.) New York: Wiley, 1978. Chapter 2, pp. 31–73.
5. Jones, Ernest. *The Life and Work of Sigmund Freud.* (Abridged ed.) New York: Basic Books, 1961. (Also in paperbound edition by Anchor Books.)
6. Kline, Paul. *Psychology and Freudian Theory.* New York: Methuen, 1984. (Paperbound.)
7. Menninger, Karl. *Theory of Psychoanalytic Technique.* New York: Basic Books, 1958. (Also in paperbound edition by Harper & Row.)

8. Pervin, Lawrence A. *Personality: Theory and Research.* (4th ed.) New York: Wiley, 1984. Chapters 3 and 4, pp. 61–146.

9. Strupp. Hans H. Freudian analysis today. *Psychology Today,* July 1972, pp. 33–40.

B. F. Skinner
and
Radical Behaviorism

■   **BIOGRAPHICAL SKETCH OF SKINNER**   ■

Burrhus Frederic Skinner was born in 1904 in Susquehanna, Pennsylvania, where he was raised in a warm, stable family environment. His father was a lawyer; his mother, according to Skinner's description, was "bright and beautiful," with rigid, unchanging standards of what was "right." While growing up, Skinner was an avid builder of things—scooters, wagons, sleds, rafts, seesaws, slingshots, blowguns, model airplanes, and so on. He even tried to build a glider in which to fly and worked unsuccessfully on a perpetual-motion machine.

After graduating from a small high school that he claims he liked, Skinner went on to Hamilton College (a small liberal arts school in New York State). There he majored in English and served as a tutor in a family from whom he acquired a heightened appreciation of music, art, writing, and the "art of living." He also became involved in various troublemaking activities: he helped perpetrate a hoax involving a scheduled visit to the college by Charlie Chaplin, the famous movie actor and comedian (a large crowd gathered in vain); he attacked Phi Beta Kappa in a student publication; and he and a group of other students created such a disturbance at commencement exercises that they were reprimanded by the college president.

After college he attempted to make his mark as a writer. During the next two years he became discouraged with writing, discovered that he was interested in psychology (partly because of reading about early behavioristic ideas), lived in Greenwich Village for several months, and spent a summer in Europe. In the fall of 1928, Skinner entered Harvard University and began studying psychology.

After getting a Ph.D. in 1931, he stayed on at Harvard for five years doing research. He then took a teaching position at the University of Minnesota. In 1945 he became Chairman of the Department of Psychology at Indiana University, and in 1948 he returned to Harvard as a professor. He was married in 1936; he and his wife have two daughters.

Skinner's first important book was *The Behavior of Organisms*, published in 1938. Among his later works are *Walden Two* (1948), *Science and Human Behavior* (1953), *Verbal Behavior* (1957), *The Technology of Teaching* (1968), *Contingencies of Reinforcement* (1969), *Beyond Freedom and Dignity* (1971), *About Behaviorism* (1974), *Reflections on Behaviorism and Society* (1978), and (with M. E. Vaughan) *Enjoy Old Age* (1983).

■   RADICAL BEHAVIORISM   ■

Because he is such an insistent and influential spokesman for behaviorism, B. F. Skinner can be considered the contemporary successor to John B. Watson, founder of the behavioristic approach to psychology. In 1912 Watson, a Johns Hopkins University professor, began to espouse a point of view about the study of humans that was to resound throughout the field of psychology. His most important book, *Psychology from the Standpoint of a Behaviorist*, was published in 1919. He was vehement in his assertion that psychology should not be a science of the mind but rather a science of behavior. He showed great impatience with the techniques of introspection being used by psychologists to investigate conscious states; also, he criticized the complexity and vagueness of psychoanalytic interpretations of human behavior. To understand humans, Watson insisted, psychology must focus on the study of observable conditions and not get lost in speculations about inner, unobservable states of mind; psychology must be objective and avoid falling into subjective approaches.

Watson sometimes made extreme statements; for example, he said that he could take any healthy infant and make it into whatever was desired—doctor, lawyer, artist, beggar, or thief—by providing the proper environment. An inference frequently drawn from his comment is that he completely ignored genetic factors (although this is not actually true). Also, his explanation of thinking as subvocal speech implied that he didn't really accept the phenomenon of thought. These kinds of statements have resulted in Watson's being considered an extreme environmentalist.

Though Skinner is similar to Watson in his strong advocacy of the advantages of an objective behavioral approach, he believes that Watson's more extreme statements have helped to create some wrong impressions of behaviorism. As Skinner has made clear, especially in his book *About Behaviorism* (1974), modern radical behaviorism (1) *does* consider feelings, thoughts, and other inner events, though not as causes of behavior; (2) *does* acknowledge the importance of genetic endowment in determining aspects of behavior; and (3) *does* consider topics such as self-knowledge and creativity, though not in the traditional ways.

It must be emphasized that, while acknowledging that humans are feeling and thinking organisms, Skinner does not look within the human psyche for any of the *causes* of behavior, and he denies the necessity of postulating states of mind or internal motives *for explanatory purposes.* It is perhaps in this sense that Skinner's behaviorism most deservedly can be termed "radical." His approach is also radical because he applies the same type of analysis to covert behaviors occurring "within the skin" (that is, feelings, thoughts, and so on) as he does to overt, publicly observable behaviors.

Skinner stresses the importance of discovering *functional relations* (or, informally expressed, "cause-and-effect connections") between environmental conditions and behaviors. He has made a special contribution by repeatedly pointing out that the social and physical conditions of our environments are critically important in determining our behaviors. He proposes that much behavioral control is exerted by observable factors that can be sought out and specified in objective and detailed terms. Importantly, he believes that this control extends to the internal behaviors of feeling and thinking, as well as applying to external actions.

In the process of investigating the effects of environmental conditions on behavior, Skinner and his colleagues have developed sophisticated research techniques, collected a huge amount of scientific data, and come up with a number of significant behavioral concepts. Radical behaviorists are able to describe with considerable detail various observable factors that affect learning, thereby buttressing their arguments that human behavior is controlled in many ways by circumstances that can be objectively specified and manipulated.

Many contemporary psychologists are moderate behaviorists, holding some midposition when attempting to explain human functioning. They tend to include certain internal determinants, such as attitudes, cognitive processes, and motives, while also focusing on determinants in the social and physical environments. To a limited extent, even psychoanalysts are behavioristic. They do observe behavior, as when they listen to (observe) patients' free associations and descriptions of dreams (verbal behaviors); also, they believe in the importance of certain environmental factors, such as traumatic events during early childhood. They go off the behavioristic track, however, when they move the explanation for their patients' problems inside the person and attribute these problems to some internal cause, such as an unresolved Oedipus complex, an overly strict superego, repressed impulses, or other psychodynamic conflicts or forces.

■   RADICAL DETERMINISM   ■

Being a thoroughgoing behaviorist, Skinner is also a *radical determinist.* He acknowledges Freud's contribution to deterministic thinking in Western psychology: Freud emphasized that human behavior is lawful and not accidental; that is, there are causes for everything we do. Skinner agrees with this position. However, he is also critical of Freud, pointing out that the explanations suggested by psychoanalytic theory are often confused because of the insertion of some mentalistic concept between the behavior and the antecedent causal event. For example, a father may severely punish his young son for masturbating, causing the boy to have later problems in his sexual behavior. The cause-and-effect relationship, according to Skinner, need include only a description of the punishing event and the abnormal sexual behavior. Why relate the sexual problem to guilt or anxiety? What is gained by inserting these sorts of concepts? If used, they too have to be explained; in other words, where does the anxiety or guilt come from? To answer this, one is forced back to environmental events.

Skinner says that mentalistic concepts only confuse and mislead, drawing attention away from real causes, such as punishment. A further danger is that concepts such as guilt and anxiety may come to assume a role that is too important and concrete. They may then be used in and of themselves to explain behavior, and the actual environmental circumstances that brought about the behavior may be ignored. Skinner says that such concepts are *explanatory fictions;* they are used for explanatory purposes but in fact explain nothing. He gives no ground to mentalistic explanations in his psychology. He takes a strong deterministic stand, firmly committing himself to the search for observable causes of behavior.

In Skinner's view, there also is no place in scientific psychology for an assumption that human behavior is governed by "individual choice" as that phrase is commonly used. He argues against traditional conceptualizations of persons as free agents who decide their own fates. Rather, the individual's behavior (his or her "personality") is determined by past and present events in the objective world of which he or she is a part.

It is important to realize that Skinner does not deny that innate, hereditary factors contribute to aspects of behavior. For example, genetic endowment determines the general range of responses of which we are capable and also is influential in determining that certain outcomes strengthen the behaviors they follow. He points out, however, that, if genetic endowment is to be explained, it is the environment once again that must be considered. He indicates that "contingencies of survival" determine what is hereditary for a given species (that is, the environment serves to select those behaviors that allow survival). If environmental conditions remain sufficiently constant for a prolonged period, those members of the species who behave in the particular ways that allow survival in this environment will be the ones who reproduce; in this way a species comes to have certain genetic characteristics. But it must be remembered that it is the environment that has had, and continues to have, control over this process.

Skinner warns against attributing particular behaviors to "instincts," because this explanation tends to ignore the causative role played by the environment. He also cautions against quickly assigning the cause of a person's behavior to genetic endowment; there may be an explanation in terms of the particular conditions to which the individual has been exposed during his or her own lifetime.

The effects of exposure to various events during one's life span are critically important in Skinnerian psychology. It is assumed that information about the relationships between such events and the resultant behaviors is essential to an adequate account of a person's functioning. Skinner suggests strongly that if genetic factors could be clearly specified and if neurophysiological processes were known in detail (and Skinner views these as worthwhile pursuits for other researchers), this would not rule out the necessity for the scientific analysis of the effects of environmental factors on behavior. Environmental manipulation, in Skinner's view, provides the key to improving human behavior.

In brief, then, Skinner has indicated that both genetic makeup *and* personal history are responsible for an individual's behavior, but his own study has concentrated on the latter by emphasizing the effects of objective, observable conditions in the environment. He believes that full knowledge of these two sets of factors (genetic and environmental) would allow a complete account of human behavior. If Skinner's prescriptions were followed, such knowledge would be pursued with vigor; mentalistic concepts that impede progress would be cast aside, never again to darken the door of science.

■ SOURCES OF DATA ■

Skinner's ideas developed and were nurtured through close contact with the experimental laboratory. He and his colleagues have conducted study after study under carefully controlled laboratory conditions, typically using rats or pigeons as subjects, in attempts to collect data relevant to conditioning processes. The concepts of behavior that are associated with Skinnerian thinking can be traced to findings derived from these studies. There has been a consistent emphasis on the collection of precise, quantitative data.

The so-called Skinner box (a term that Skinner himself does not endorse) provides one means for the type of controlled observation that is at the heart of radical behaviorism. This device is a small chamber in which an animal can be isolated from the external environment and subjected to conditions specifically created by the experimenter. The behavior that is typically studied is lever pressing by rats or key pecking by pigeons (the term "key" refers to a disc or other device that, when sufficient pressure is applied, triggers a food dispenser); responses are usually recorded electromechanically, and rates of response under various conditions provide the data of primary interest.[1] For example, the experimenter is often interested in observing changes in response rate when the time of presentation of some reinforcer, such as food, is varied, or when an aversive stimulus, such as an electric shock, is applied or withdrawn as a consequence of the animal's responses.

You may be asking at this point "What can such studies have to do with *human* behavior?" After all, *we* are not isolated from the real world, and our most important and interesting behaviors do not involve pressing levers or performing other such simple responses. The answer to this question is found in the observations that Skinner and his followers have made when concepts derived from relatively "artificial" laboratory experiments with lower animals have been applied to humans. Such applications are called by various terms, including "behavior modification," "behavioral engineering," and "applied behavior analysis." Skinnerian concepts have been effectively applied in such areas as (1) student performance (Skinner has been a pioneer in the development of programmed instruction, teaching machines, and other educational innovations); (2) the treatment of autistic children, retarded persons, and psychotics; (3) industrial management; and (4) behavior therapy for problem behaviors.

Another question might be "Why not simply study humans to begin with, instead of doing research with animals such as rats and pigeons?" A number of studies *have* been done at the human level; efforts by behaviorists to arrive at fundamental behavioral concepts have not been limited to the use of lower animals. However, the relative simplicity of lower organisms, and the fact that the environments of these organisms can be controlled by the experimenter to a much greater extent

---

[1]The use of rates of response as basic data reflects Skinner's view that numerous assumptions made about organisms—humans as well as lower animals—are based on the frequency with which they perform specific acts. For example, when we say that a given person has a particular "habit" or "attitude," or that he or she is "enthusiastic" or "very interested," we are generally basing these statements on observations that this person *often* behaves in certain ways. Therefore it is critical to study the conditions that determine changes in the rate of performing various behaviors.

than is the case with human experimental subjects, have made them the frequent choice for basic research projects.

Although some persons object to the drawing of concepts of behavior from "artificial" laboratory experiments (especially if animals are used), this criticism loses its force when the validity of these concepts is tested in actual, real-life situations. Studying the relatively simple responses of lower animals under carefully controlled conditions often allows the formulation of very basic behavioral concepts that can then be applied and tested at the human level in the real world. This is what Skinner and his colleagues have done, often with a great deal of success.

Some of Skinner's generalizations are more difficult than others to test. For example, one of his great interests has been to suggest plans for improved social structures. His novel, *Walden Two*, is an expression of this interest. It is a description of a utopian community in which his basic laboratory-derived ideas are put into effect. An actual community (Twin Oaks, near Louisa, Virginia) was formed in 1967 by a small group of persons (not including Skinner) interested in putting *Walden Two*'s ideas into practice; with various modifications, the community has survived.[2] The extent to which Skinner's ideas would work in other community settings on a larger scale is an open question.

In his 1971 book of social criticism, *Beyond Freedom and Dignity*, Skinner also goes far out on a limb to suggest drastic changes that he feels are necessary if our society is to survive and flourish. To create these changes in our social institutions and practices, under carefully controlled conditions that would allow precisely measured effects, would certainly be an interesting examination of the generality of Skinner's concepts. However, the likelihood of this possibility is not strong. Too many people are unnerved by his extreme emphasis on environmental determinants of human behavior and by his exclusion of such traditional concepts as free will and individual autonomy (more will be said about this later).

■   **RESPONDENT BEHAVIOR**   ■

We will now get more specific about the concepts applied by Skinner in his analysis of behavior. He distinguishes between two general categories of behavior: *respondent* and *operant*. In this section we will briefly discuss the former; the latter is far more important in Skinnerian psychology and will be discussed in the next section.

The term "respondent" refers to a *specific kind of behavior that is elicited by a specific kind of stimulus*. It indicates a reflexive-type

[2]See Kathleen Kinkade's *A Walden Two Experiment: The First Five Years of Twin Oaks Community* (New York: William Morrow, 1972). Portions of this book appeared in the January 1973 and February 1973 issues of *Psychology Today*.

response, and the stimulus precedes the behavior. For example, changes in light intensity cause the pupillary reflex, a sharp puff of air directed at the eye causes a blinking response, a tap on the patellar tendon causes the knee reflex, and contact with a sharp object causes a withdrawal response. Another example, familiar to all psychologists and many laypersons, can be found in Ivan Pavlov's work with dogs. This noted Russian physiologist is famous for his studies, in the early 1900s, of classical-conditioning processes (Skinner uses the term "respondent conditioning" instead of "classical conditioning," which is commonly used by non-Skinnerians). Basic to Pavlov's observations is the fact that the placement of food in a dog's mouth causes the animal to salivate (this salivation reflex is respondent behavior, in Skinner's terms). When the presentation of food is paired repeatedly with some originally neutral stimulus, such as the sound of a bell, the dog eventually begins to salivate to the sound of the bell alone, without the presentation of food. Thus, respondent conditioning has occured.[3] Of course, if the bell were then sounded a number of times but never again paired with food, the salivation response would gradually diminish and eventually disappear. This process is called *extinction*.

A study by John Watson and Rosalie Rayner (*Journal of Experimental Psychology*, Vol. 3, February 1920) illustrates that Pavlovian conditioning principles apply to human, as well as animal, learning. They conditioned an 11-month-old boy named Albert to fear a white rat by repeatedly presenting the rat at the same time as they created a loud noise (by striking a hammer against a steel bar). They knew beforehand, by testing, that the loud noise elicited a fear reaction (a respondent behavior) from Albert. Thus, through pairing of the loud noise and the white rat (to which the boy initially showed no fear), the white rat finally came to elicit fear responses.

A phenomenon called *stimulus generalization* also occurred. Albert not only came to fear the white rat, but he also began to show fear in the presence of similar stimuli, such as a rabbit, a dog, and a fur coat. The significance of this finding is that learning experiences may result in emotional responses to whole classes of stimuli. Watson and Rayner's study makes clear the possibility that seemingly "irrational" fears and emotions may have their origin in respondent-conditioning situations. A child bitten by a dog ("neutral" dog paired with a painful bite) may then fear all dogs; the person who experiences pain in a dentist's office ("neutral" office paired with painful drilling) may then fear not

---

[3]In common *classical-conditioning terminology*, the food is called an *unconditioned stimulus*; it elicits the *unconditioned response* of salivation. The assumption is that this is an innate, rather than a learned, connection between a stimulus and a response. The originally neutral stimulus, the bell, is called a *conditioned stimulus* because it eventually elicits, by itself, the *conditioned response* of salivation. This connection is learned.

only that office but also similar offices, such as might be encountered when he or she changes dentists.

The point to be stressed here is that *respondent behavior can be conditioned.* An originally neutral stimulus (for example, a bell or a white rat) can be made to elicit a particular behavior (for example, salivation or fearfulness) by being associated with a stimulus (for example, food or a loud noise) that already elicits that behavior. The following diagram attempts to sum up and clarify the process of respondent conditioning; the respondent behavior is salivation. (A word of caution is in order: although the bell comes to elicit salivation after being paired repeatedly with food, it does not become qualitatively identical to the food. As mentioned previously, if the bell is presented alone time after time, never being paired again with food, *extinction* occurs; that is, the salivation response gradually decreases in intensity.)

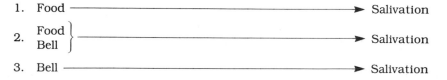

1. Food ——————————————————————→ Salivation
2. Food ⎱
   Bell ⎰ ——————————————————————→ Salivation
3. Bell ——————————————————————→ Salivation

Skinner acknowledges this type of conditioning in which a conditioned stimulus *precedes* and *elicits* a conditioned response. However, he believes that the most significant and complex behaviors are *not* merely conditioned reflexive responses to specific stimuli; rather, they are responses that are *emitted* and that produce consequences. He is much more interested in the *active* organism than in the relatively *passive* organism emphasized in respondent conditioning. In his emphasis on operant conditioning, Skinner differs from Watson, who gave a great deal of attention to reflexive-type, stimulus-response relationships.

■ OPERANT BEHAVIOR ■

Operant behavior is *behavior that operates on the environment to produce consequences.* It is emitted rather than elicited behavior, and it is characteristic of an *active* organism. To Skinner, the study of emitted responses and their consequences constitutes the essential subject matter of psychology. Whereas respondent behavior is under the direct control of its antecedents, operant behavior is initially produced by an organism in the absence of any easily identifiable eliciting stimulus and is controlled by its consequences (the effects that it has).

Respondent behaviors such as eye blinks, knee jerks, salivation, and certain fear responses can be contrasted with operant behaviors such as reading, writing, playing a musical instrument, eating with a knife and fork, and driving a car. Operant behaviors constitute most of the significant responses that define us as individuals. There are differences among individuals in their behaviors (each person has his or her own "personality"), and operant-conditioning concepts help to explain these differences.

What consequences can an emitted behavior have? The most important consequence in Skinner's analysis of behavior is *reinforcement.* If a behavior is *reinforced,* it is strengthened: the probability *increases* that that type of behavior will be repeated in similar circumstances in the future. It is essential to realize that this does not necessarily mean that exactly the same behavior will be repeated; a similar behavior having the given effect may occur. A whole class, or set, of behaviors, not simply the speific response, is strengthened by reinforcement. (Skinner uses the term "operant" to refer to a class of responses that produce certain consequences.)

A distinction must be made between "reinforcement" and "reward." Behavior that is *reinforced* is strengthened, whereas behavior that is *rewarded* may or may not be strengthened. Skinner explains that something is a reinforcer *only* when it actually strengthens the behavior that produces it; in other words, reinforcers are defined by their effects. What is reinforcing may vary, depending on the person, the behavior, and the situation. The notion of reward does not include the strengthening effect explicit in the concept of reinforcement. Rewards such as prizes, money, and so on sometimes do strengthen the behaviors they follow (in which case they are also reinforcers), but they don't always do so.

Perhaps reinforcement, which is the essence of *operant conditioning,* seems very simple; however, its ramifications are far-reaching and dramatic. Essentially, Skinner would consider a newborn infant to be a behavior emitter, and, as the infant matures, he or she becomes capable of producing a wide variety of responses. Some of these responses have consequences that are reinforcing, and some do not. For example, certain responses allow one to successfully ride a bicycle, but others are unsuccessful; the former are thus reinforced, whereas the latter are not. Many responses (for example, speaking, eating, or dressing in accepted ways) are reinforced by the approval and praise of parents, teachers, peers, and others; these social reinforcers are very important in conditioning behavior. In brief, then, responses that are reinforced tend to be repeated, increasing in frequency and becoming established as common responses in the person's behavior repertoire. These responses constitute *conditioned behavior.*

An interesting development occurs when the connection between a response and the reinforcer that follows it is an accidental one. In such cases, there is no actual cause-and-effect relationship between the response and the reinforcer. Skinner calls responses conditioned in this way *superstitious behavior* and points out that human behavior is "heavily superstitious."[4] The rain dances performed by some groups of people provide dramatic examples of superstitious behavior. The occasional chance occurrence of rain after such an appeal reinforces the dancing sufficiently to cause it to continue.

Everyday instances of superstitious behavior are numerous. A common example can be observed when a group of persons is waiting for a self-operated elevator; often someone begins pushing the button repeatedly despite the fact that the elevator light is already "on," signaling that the button has *already* been pushed. This behavior has probably been reinforced several times by the chance arrival of the elevator just after repeated button pushing. The person very likely would admit that repeated pressing is actually unnecessary and has no real effect; nevertheless, the behavior persists. Many people have an elaborate set of behaviors for starting their cars on cold days, despite the fact that only a couple of these responses are actually effective; yet, because the car has started in the past (providing reinforcement) after the performance of these behaviors, the routine is continued. Athletes often show superstitious behaviors; baseball players at bat may go through a ritual (hitching up their pants, touching the plate with the end of the bat, kicking dirt, and so on) that is sometimes followed by getting a hit; therefore the ritual is repeated time and again.

Behaviors that are ignored or that produce no reinforcing consequences tend not to increase in frequency—that is, they are not strengthened. A child would not be likely to learn to read if she or he were never reinforced with praise or attention for attempts to read; a college student probably would not become "politically involved" if an audience were never gained for his or her ideas; a business executive would be unlikely to continue a procedure that was not having the effect of increasing business.

Also, if conditioned behavior (previously reinforced behavior) no longer results in reinforcement, it tends to become less and less frequent. This process is called *operant extinction*. For example, a child who has been conditioned to speak quietly at home, through parental reinforcement of this behavior, may continue to do so on initial trips to the local playground. However, if other children do not respond to (do not rein-

---

[4]Superstitious behavior has been illustrated vividly in the laboratory. A pigeon is placed in a Skinner box, and food is delivered every 15 seconds, regardless of what the bird is doing at the time. Whatever behavior is being emitted when the reinforcer (food) arrives will tend to increase in frequency. Before long, the pigeon is performing the behavior at a high rate. Skinner has found that various responses have been conditioned in this way, including turning in a circle, hopping from foot to foot, and lifting the head.

force) this quiet talking, it will gradually disappear (extinguish) in the child's playground interactions—perhaps to be replaced by shouting and loud chatter, which do get attention (reinforcement) from peers.

In Skinnerian psychology, "personality" is considered to be primarily the result of the individual's *personal history of reinforcement.* (Though genetic endowment also plays a role, reinforcements determine the specific behaviors that are shaped and maintained and that are typical for the individual.) Contrast the man who is very argumentative and engages in physical violence with the man who is affable and nonviolent. How did these differences in behavior come about? Skinner's concepts suggest that the critical factor is different histories of reinforcement. The former person's aggressive behaviors may have been encouraged and praised (positively reinforced) by his parents or peers; also, in the environment in which he typically operates, these behaviors are probably successful and therefore are positively reinforced adaptations. In addition, negative reinforcement (to be explained more fully shortly) has probably operated to increase his aggressive behaviors. That is, aggression may have effectively removed him from uncomfortable or dangerous situations, as when punching an annoying or threatening person has resulted in a cessation of the annoyances or threats.

The affable, nonviolent person's experiences very likely have been such that pleasant, nonaggressive behaviors have been reinforced, and his present environment continues to maintain these kinds of behaviors. An assumption in Skinnerian psychology is that both these individuals (barring significant genetic differences or defects) would have been capable of developing either set of behaviors. Different reinforcement contingencies resulted in the actual behaviors that become typical for each person.

A point that is often missed by those who are freshly introduced to operant-conditioning concepts is that reinforcements often are subtle. In other words, it is not always easy to find the significant reinforcing events in a person's life history. For example, identical twins raised in the same family environment may turn out to be quite different in their behaviors as adults. In such cases it is tempting to think that something mysterious and unexplainable has occurred; it seems that both persons were exposed to the same environment and the same events. How could they turn out differently? The explanation is not to be found by taking into account only the *general* characteristics of their reinforcement histories; *detailed* information would be necessary if the behavioral differences were to be understood. If specific details could be obtained, there would be a number of instances in the personal histories of each twin when emitted behaviors and the consequences of these behaviors differed from those of the other twin. It is impossible to imagine a case in which two individuals, even identical twins, have produced *exactly* the same behaviors with *exactly* the same consequences. Therefore, no two individuals have *exactly* the same "personality," although of course there may be many similarities due to histories of reinforcement that are approximately (even if not precisely) the same.

Skinner indicates that there are two types of reinforcement—*positive reinforcement* and *negative reinforcement*—that can occur as a consequence of behavior. *Both types increase the probability of response*—that is, they both strengthen behavior. Positive reinforcement involves the *addition* of something (a positive reinforcer) to a situation when a response is made. For example, a response may be positively reinforced if the obtaining of food, water, sexual contact, money, or praise is a consequence. Negative reinforcement involves the *removal* of something (called either a negative reinforcer *or* an aversive stimulus) from a situation when a response is made. For example, a response may be negatively reinforced if the removal of extreme cold or heat, a loud noise, a threat, a tedious task, or a headache is a consequence. In short, much of our behavior is conditioned because it gains us something (in the case of positive reinforcement) or because it allows us to escape or avoid something (in the case of negative reinforcement).

Skinner's terms "positive" and "negative" should not be thought of as having the same meanings that they typically have in everyday life. For example, rejection by an admired person typically would be considered negative, but such rejection actually may increase one's approaches to that person (perhaps rejection is better than being ignored completely). If rejection has the effect of strengthening approach responses, it is then considered a *positive* reinforcer.

Similarly, negative reinforcers are not always stimuli or events that commonly would be considered "negative." For example, overt displays of parental affection toward a teenage son actually may be *negative* reinforcers (especially if they occur in front of his friends). Therefore, offensive behaviors by the son may be strengthened if they remove the parent's affectionate responses. Again, the important point is that positive and negative reinforcers are defined by their effects, not by popular conceptions.

Something cannot be considered a positive reinforcer or a negative reinforcer (aversive stimulus) until its effects have been observed. Before calling something a positive reinforcer, it must be determined that its *addition* does increase the probability of response; for a negative reinforcer, its *removal* must be observed to increase the probability of response. This sort of explicit specificity prevents confusion when attempting to predict and control behavior.

A sloppy interpretation of Skinnerian concepts can be very misleading. We should not assume, for instance, that haphazardly applied reinforcers will be effective or that the same things will be reinforcing in all cases for all individuals. As an example, parents sometimes are incapable of understanding and dealing with their children's "offensive and irresponsible" behaviors. They may say something like this: "We've given our children the best clothes, plenty of money, the use of the family car, and we send them to good, private schools. How could they turn out this way?" The indirectly expressed assumption here seems to be that, with all these "positive reinforcers," the children should be behaving in accordance with the parents' wishes. A vague knowledge of operant conditioning might lead them to believe that Skinner is dead wrong and that positive reinforcement doesn't work. A more complete knowledge of operant conditioning would help clarify the situation. Perhaps the clothes, money, and so on are not made contingent on "desirable" behaviors; that is, maybe the parents simply provide everything for the children without supplying the reinforcers as a consequence of certain behaviors. Another possibility is that at least some of these things are not really positive reinforcers; "the best clothes" or "good, private schools" may be effective reinforcers for the parents but not for the children. Also, the children's "offensive and irresponsible" behaviors may be strongly positively reinforced by the approval of their peers.

The implications of negative reinforcement also are very significant for everyday situations, and an adequate grasp of this concept can elucidate many problems of behavior control. Skinner himself is an advocate of positive reinforcement; he believes that conditions are best when our actions gain us something and that it is less desirable to do things in order to escape from something (as in the case of negative reinforcement). Some situations are loaded with negative reinforcers. In certain school systems, for instance, the academic work is so dull and dreary that any behavior that removes a child from having to do this work is highly negatively reinforced. Remember the effect of negative reinforcement: *a behavior that removes a negative reinforcer tends to increase in frequency.* If cutting classes, daydreaming during lectures, or creating havoc in the classroom remove the child from an aversive learning situation (a negative reinforcer), then these behaviors can be expected to increase; the child will be conditioned to emit these behaviors regularly. A similar situation exists on many boring and tedious jobs. Employees may be conditioned to escape from this type of work (a negative reinforcer) by taking extended coffee breaks, sustaining injuries, being absent, or simply quitting. Reinforcement, both positive and negative, provides the key to much human behavior.

To explain the vast range of human behavior that is subject to control by reinforcement, Skinner refers to *conditioned reinforcers*—for example, money, academic grades, attention, approval, and affection. These conditioned reinforcers are initially paired with *primary reinforcers* such as food and sexual contact. Money is associated with the provision of many necessities (primary reinforcers), and school grades are also associated, though less directly, with the attainment of primary reinforcers (passing grades lead to a diploma, which leads to a job, which leads to self-support, which leads to independence, the ability to purchase food and other necessities, and the ability to attract a marriage partner).

Attention, approval, and affection from others become conditioned reinforcers because of their association with the provision of primary reinforcers by other persons. For example, parents who give approval and attention to their children also provide primary reinforcers such as food, warmth, cuddling, and so on. In addition, signs of attention, approval, and affection from members of the opposite sex are likely to be associated with sexual contacts. The main point here is that a whole variety of stimuli can attain reinforcing properties through their associations with primary reinforcers, and these conditioned reinforcers can then operate independently to control behavior. The types of conditioned reinforcers we have discussed here are called *generalized reinforcers;* they are associated with more than one primary reinforcer. (It should be mentioned that it sometimes is argued that attention, approval, and affection are more than conditioned reinforcers; they also may have some characteristics of primary reinforcers—that is, they may be related to basic biological factors.)

A very important reinforcer that affects human behavior is success in manipulating the environment. Skinner indicates that simply "being effective" or "being right" may reinforce behavior, and he suggests that the human capacity to be reinforced in this way may have its roots in our evolutionary history. That is, part of the effectiveness of this reinforcer may be unconditioned; perhaps the survival value of successful environmental manipulations has resulted (through evolution) in the tendency for human behavior to be reinforced by these types of consequences. He gives the example of the baby who repeatedly shakes a rattle; apparently the simple effect created by this behavior is reinforcing. This notion is very significant, since it means that we perhaps engage in a great deal of behavior partly because it produces some change in our environment. Of course, primary reinforcers may also be involved; food, water, sexual contact, and so on often are obtained only through successful manipulations of the environment.

Another way in which behavior is controlled, or in which control is attempted, is through *punishment.* Skinner believes that the effectiveness of this technique is limited and that it is an undesirable means of control. He defines two cases of punishment, both occurring as a consequence of behavior. In one case a *negative reinforcer is presented* after a response, and in the other case a *positive reinforcer is removed* after a response. The first case can be illustrated by some common situations: slapping or scolding a child for misbehavior, berating a worker who has made a mistake, or fining a driver who has violated the speed limit. Examples of the second case include taking away a teenager's driving privileges for "talking back," sending a child to his or her room during dinner for displaying bad table manners, deducting money from an employee's paycheck for being late, or walking away from a person who brings up a topic you don't want to talk about.

The term "punishment" is used appropriately only if a *known* negative reinforcer is presented or if a *known* positive reinforcer is removed. It is not sufficient simply to *assume* that some event will be punishing. A common result of punishment is the *suppression* (at least temporarily) of the type of behavior that precedes it; however, many *intended* punishments do not accomplish this goal. For example, students put on detention often continue to be disruptive in class, criminals put into jail often commit crimes again, and employees who are reprimanded often continue to perform poorly; the actions taken in these cases are not effective and therefore should not be considered "punishments." In fact, some circumstances commonly thought to be punishing may actually result in the reinforcement of undesirable behaviors. The student sent to the principal's office may gain the admiration of classmates for being "tough" or "brave" and therefore the types of behaviors that result in expulsion from the classroom may increase; the person who goes to jail may find acceptance and approval among fellow prisoners for antisocial behaviors and therefore these behaviors may be even more likely to occur after imprisonment (but perhaps with more caution about getting caught); the worker who is yelled at by his or her boss may gain the attention and sympathy of fellow employees who resent oppressive working conditions, which might result in further mistakes on the job.

More will be said about Skinner's views on punishment in a later section. Be aware, however, that Skinner differentiates between "negative reinforcement," in which an aversive stimulus is removed, resulting in an *increase* in the probability of the kind of behavior that preceded its removal, and "punishment," in which an aversive stimulus is added or a positive reinforcer is removed, generally resulting in at least temporary *suppression* of behavior. These two behavior-control techniques are commonly confused by persons newly acquainted with Skinnerian psychology, probably because the term "negative reinforcement" seems to imply a situation that is "not reinforcing." This is not the case, however, in Skinner's usage.

We need now to return briefly to a discussion of "stimuli." Remember that in respondent conditioning a specific stimulus *elicits* a response. We said that this is not the case in operant conditioning, since operant behavior is *emitted* rather than elicited. However, operant behavior does come to be affected by certain stimuli. For example, a pigeon may be exposed to a situation in a Skinner box in which key pecking is reinforced only when a light is on. When the light is off, pecking does not result in reinforcement. Eventually, the pigeon will peck only when the light is on; also, the light's being on will result in pecking behavior.

The light has become a *discriminative stimulus*, and it exerts a kind of control over pecking behavior. The establishment of this relationship between a stimulus and a response is not the same as in respondent conditioning. Pecking was initially an *emitted* behavior; it was *not elicited* by any specifiable stimulus. Only after the pecking was emitted by the pigeon and then reinforced in the presence of the light did it come to bear any relation to the light stimulus. When a response is likely to occur in the presence of particular stimuli because of the availability of reinforcement at that time, a *discrimination* has been established. For example, a child eventually learns to call "mommy" and "daddy" only in the presence of his or her parents because their presence is associated with reinforcement for those verbal responses (that is, they give approval or attention).[5]

We are conditioned to make many discriminations in everyday life, from those that are relatively trivial to those that are crucial, such as proceeding on a green, but not red, light when we are driving. Banana eating is controlled in part by the yellowness of bananas; eating them when they are a particular shade of yellow has been reinforced (they tasted good). Our approaches to strangers are determined partially by their facial expressions; approaches often are reinforced (we are "accepted") by smiling strangers but not by scowling strangers. Opening the door is controlled by the ringing of the doorbell; making this response when the bell rings has been followed by reinforcement in the past (someone has been at the door). Going to the mailbox is controlled by the time; this behavior is followed by reinforcement (the mail is there) when we go at a particular time. In the preceding cases the discriminative stimuli are a particular shade of yellow, a smile or a scowl, a ringing doorbell, and a particular time, respectively. Other illustrations of discrimination could be given, and each would be an example of how the environment exerts an influence on our behavior. Skinner has elucidated important aspects of environmental control through discrimination and the other concepts discussed in this section. The

---

[5]*Induction* (or generalization) and *discrimination* are related concepts in Skinner's psychology. Induction refers to the fact that, when behavior comes under the control of a particular stimulus, it is also controlled by other stimuli with similar properties. If we are reinforced for responding in the presence of a particular stimulus, we will also tend to respond in a similar (but probably not identical) way to similar stimuli. This concept accounts for the fact that we do not have to be conditioned to respond appropriately to every "new" situation we meet. Since many situations have certain common properties, our behavior generalizes to these situations. For example, a person who can drive one car can also drive other cars. Also, the person who has been reinforced in one social situation for responding in a certain way will make similar responses in another similar social situation. Obviously, induction has its advantages.

Discriminations are also essential, however. If discriminations didn't exist, inappropriate responses would often occur. The reinforcement of certain responses and the extinction of others in the presence of different stimuli bring about discriminations.

argument has been strengthened that environmental factors, rather than "inner dynamics," determine our behaviors.

The following are some of the highlights of this section:

1. *Operant behavior* is emitted and is affected by its consequences.
2. The most significant consequence of operant behavior is *reinforcement* (either positive or negative), which results in the strengthening of behavior. This process is called *operant conditioning.*
3. *Conditioned* (reinforced) *behaviors* constitute the typical responses in our behavior repertoires.
4. *Superstitious behaviors* are the results of accidental relationships between responses and reinforcers.
5. We make many responses that are not reinforced, and therefore they decrease in strength; that is, they undergo *extinction.*
6. Our unique "personalities" result mainly from our *individual histories of reinforcement.*
7. Many *conditioned reinforcers,* such as money, affect our behavior. These reinforcers gain their influence by being associated with *primary reinforcers,* such as food.
8. *Punishment* is a behavior-control technique designed to suppress behavior. (Skinner opposes its use.)
9. *Discrimination* results when reinforcement is available only in the presence of a particular stimulus (or particular stimuli).

■ THE SHAPING OF BEHAVIOR ■

Skinner suggests an analogy between the way operant conditioning *shapes* behavior and the way a sculptor shapes a piece of clay. Operant behaviors such as bar pressing for food by a rat in a Skinner box or reading and writing by a student in a classroom do not emerge full-blown. They are *shaped* in successive stages. The term "shaping" refers to the differential reinforcement of successive approximations; responses that are closer and closer to the desired response are required in order to maintain reinforcement. Consider the child who is learning to speak: at first almost any approximation to words is reinforced; later, reinforcement is no longer available for this behavior and closer approximations are necessary; finally, only fairly exact pronunciations are reinforced.

Shaping results in many desirable behaviors, such as learning to speak and write well, becoming proficient at sports, driving carefully, and performing highly refined job skills. However, it also may result in undesirable behaviors. A parent may ignore a child's quiet questioning but then respond (give reinforcement) when the child raises his or her voice. To get attention on subsequent occasions, the child may have to increasingly intensify the demands, until his or her typical behavior (inadvertently shaped by the parent) is to "make a fuss."

Campus and ghetto violence during the 1960s could also be viewed as being at least partially the result of shaping. Reasonable approaches to officials by students, Blacks, and other minority and deprived groups were often ignored. Louder demands were sometimes listened to and concessions sometimes made, but, when this intensity no longer brought sufficient reinforcement to the disadvantaged, they again heightened the level of protest, which in some cases elevated to physical violence and large-scale destructiveness. It would seem wise for those in authority to give serious attention to reasonable demands made in a moderate and nonviolent way, rather than to close their eyes and ears (giving no reinforcement) until escalation occurs and they then find themselves in the position of having to yield to (thereby giving reinforcement for) extreme, aggressive behaviors. This kind of process can go on and on— starting with the initial resistance of authorities, then yielding in the face of increased pressure, then holding back again, then yielding again when the intensity of behavior increases—until very violent and socially destructive activities have been inadvertently "shaped up."

A very positive application of shaping can be seen in education. Skinner has advocated the use of *programmed instruction,* in which subject matter is broken down into a series of small steps leading toward more and more complexity. The material is presented to the student in easily manageable portions. Because of the arrangement of the material in small sequential steps, from very simple to complex, the student is not likely to "get lost." He or she should be able to make a high proportion of correct responses to the accompanying questions (which are also programmed to increase gradually in complexity), and thereby progressively more complex responses are reinforced.

Programmed textbooks presenting material in small progressive steps have been developed, and there are also various *teaching machines* that present programmed material. (With the rapid growth of computer technology, there is great potential for developing more efficient and effective instructional aids.) Some of these machines provide conditioned reinforcers that involve more than simply getting the correct answer (although this in itself can be a very potent reinforcer). For example, a correct answer may be signaled by a flashing light and/or the sound of a bell. In this way, teaching machines shape behavior while "holding the student's interest" by quickly reinforcing every correct response. (This type of immediate, reinforcing feedback is often missing in regular classrooms, where students sometimes wait days or weeks to receive comments or grades on their exams or projects.) Because of these factors, plus the factors of the constant interaction between the machine and the student, the high rate of activity of the student, and the progression to more complex material only after the preceding material has been thoroughly understood, Skinner has suggested that teaching machines are similar to private tutors.

He also has pointed out that certain aversive conditions typically present in learning situations, as well as factors that make little or no contribution to education, can be avoided with programmed instruction. Students do not study in order to escape negative consequences such as reprimands or low grades, and each person moves ahead at his or her own pace, which reduces competitive behavior. In addition, reinforcement that is given consistently and immediately for small increments in performance is often more effective than long-range reinforcers such as "passing the course" or "getting a diploma."

The potential of teaching machines appears quite impressive. However, there are some problems. One is the development of good programs. It isn't always easy to break down the subject matter—English, history, science, or whatever—into small, meaningful, progressive units. This task often requires a great deal of effort. Once accomplished, however, the benefits seem numerous. As Skinner has suggested, we don't really know the full capabilities of humans, because environments have never been constructed that "push human achievement to its limits." Perhaps complete development of the possibilities offered by teaching machines would move us further toward the goal of full human achievement. Also, teachers benefit from teaching machines by having time for involvement in activities beyond those of "drillmasters."

Besides his interest in the shaping of behavior through the use of programmed instruction and teaching machines, Skinner is very concerned with the general state of American education. Responding to the many recent criticisms of our educational system, he suggests that reformers too often make broad and meaningless recommendations, such as suggesting that we need more commitment, a greater national effort, or some sort of imaginative, innovative change. He also believes that many specific suggestions, such as lengthening the school day or providing merit pay for teachers, are not adequate solutions.

What is needed, in Skinner's opinion, is the application of a technology of teaching based on the scientific analysis of behavior. This, in short, involves clarifying the goals of education (that is, being specific about what is to be taught), allowing each student to progress at his or her own rate, and maintaining "motivation" by providing immediate and appropriate positive reinforcers for progress. (Of course, programmed instruction and teaching machines play important roles in accomplishing these steps.) Skinner maintains that a sound technology of teaching would permit students to learn twice as much as they are learning now, without additional time or effort.

Rather than disbanding schools of education, as some critics of our school systems have suggested, Skinner advises that teachers be taught the technology that will allow them to do their jobs more effectively. He believes that teachers too often are misguided by vague and relatively useless humanistic and cognitive theories of learning. Such theories, in his view, lead teachers and others away from practical solutions to educational problems.

MAINTAINING BEHAVIOR:
■ SCHEDULES OF REINFORCEMENT ■

Reinforcements do more than shape behavior; they also *maintain* established behaviors. Current *contingencies of reinforcement*[6] must be studied if the range and complexity of a person's present activities are to be understood. We need to know the prevailing conditions under which reinforcements occur. To specify these conditions in full detail as they exist in the real world is extremely difficult in most cases, but even a cursory look at how and when reinforcements occur often reveals very significant determinants of behavior.

Some behaviors are reinforced every time they are emitted. This is called *continuous reinforcement.* Often the behaviors that are continuously reinforced are those that act on the physical environment; pushing or pulling a door has the consistent result of opening or closing it, and turning a faucet results consistently in the flow of water. These are simple examples of cases in which certain results (reinforcements) occur each time a particular response is made. Continuous reinforcement also maintains more complex physical activities; certain responses always result in successful skating, skiing, bicycle riding, writing, swimming, and so on, and therefore we continue to emit the behaviors appropriate for these accomplishments.

If the usual response-reinforcement relationship suddenly does not occur after a long period of continuous reinforcement, the result may be "disturbing," "weird," or perhaps "humorous." Skinner has suggested that the "house of mirrors" in an amusement park is an example of changed consequences of behavior. People are unaccustomed to the kind of feedback they receive from looking into these mirrors. Previously, there was a consistent, regular consequence each time a mirror was looked into. Another example of the effects of changing a continuous-reinforcement situation would be a wife who for years had hugged her husband when he came home from work but suddenly, one day, didn't provide this reinforcement. Her husband would probably say something like "What's wrong? Aren't you feeling well?" Or consider the case of an aspiring young business executive who has had all her ideas responded to favorably by her colleagues and supervisor; if her

---

[6]According to Skinner, *contingencies of reinforcement* involve the inter-relationships among "(1) the occasion upon which a response occurs, (2) the response itself, and (3) the reinforcing consequences." For more on this subject, see Skinner's *Contingencies of Reinforcement* (especially page 7), which is referenced at the end of this chapter.

next suggestion causes no favorable reaction, she might be quite taken aback. Her surprise would be less if her suggestions had been reinforced less consistently in the past. The self-doubts experienced by the "great lover" who finally does not succeed in a seduction attempt provides yet another illustration of the possible "upsetting" results of the breakdown of continuous reinforcement.

Behaviors that are maintained on a schedule of continuous reinforcement extinguish quite rapidly when reinforcers are no longer available. Extinction takes longer if a behavior is being maintained by a reinforcement schedule on which not every response is reinforced. The phrase "schedule of reinforcement" refers to the particular pattern or rule by which reinforcement occurs. If reinforcement occurs less than every time a particular type of behavior is emitted, a *schedule of intermittent reinforcement* is operating, and behavior maintained by such schedules is generally more resistant to extinction than is behavior maintained by continuous reinforcement. The "great lover" mentioned above would probably quit his or her seduction attempts more quickly than would a person who had a history of successes mixed with failures.

A pigeon whose key-pecking behavior has been reinforced continuously may peck somewhere around 50 to 200 times after the reinforcement is cut off. However, on an intermittent schedule, 4000 to 10,000 pecks may be emitted during the extinction period. Similar outcomes can be expected with regard to the extinction of human behaviors in everyday life. If a child's temper tantrums are being maintained by attention from the parents each time they occur (continuous reinforcement), and if there is no physical problem involved, then the tantrums will very likely stop relatively soon after the parents start ignoring them (extinction). However, if the tantrums are being maintained on an intermittent schedule—that is, if sometimes they receive attention and sometimes they do not—it will be harder for the parents to extinguish them. Very persistent behavior often results from schedules of intermittent reinforcement.

Much human behavior is maintained by intermittent reinforcement. This is generally true in cases in which other people are involved. We seldom find complete certainty in our interactions with others. Even our best friends don't *always* react favorably to our friendly behaviors; still, we persist. Other examples of the effectiveness of intermittent reinforcemnt abound: athletes often continue to compete even though they don't always win; writers often continue to write even when they publish only once in a great while; would-be gourmet cooks often keep trying despite the disappointing meals that occur between their successes. In short, human behaviors are in many cases maintained by reinforcements that occur only occasionally.

There are two major types of schedules of intermittent reinforcement: *interval schedules* and *ratio schedules*. Interval schedules are based on the passage of time, as when a pigeon in a Skinner box receives a food pellet for the first key-pecking response after a certain interval of time has passed. The time interval may be constant, or it may vary around some average. If the interval is unchanging (for example, if it is always a one-minute interval), then the schedule is called a *fixed-interval* (FI) schedule. If the interval varies (for example, sometimes it may be 50 seconds, sometimes 70 seconds, and so on, with an average time of one minute), then the schedule is called a *variable-interval* (VI) schedule. If the intervals are short, there will be a relatively higher overall rate of responding than when the intervals are long.

The man who picks up his mail each day at exactly 10 A.M., because the mail delivery is very regular and the man's behavior is thus always reinforced at 10 A.M., is operating on a fixed-interval schedule. Compare the behavior of this person with that of someone who is operating on a variable-interval schedule with regard to picking up his mail. Let's imagine that the mail carrier comes *on the average* at 10 A.M. but some days delivers at 9:30, some days at 10:30, and so on. (Compared with VI schedules typically used in laboratory studies, the average interval in this example is long and the variability of intervals quite restricted.) This man will probably check his mailbox when he sees that it is 9:30 and will continue to do so until he is at last reinforced (until the mail has come). A variable-interval schedule yields a more constant rate of responding than does a fixed-interval schedule. Our hypothetical person who is on the variable-interval schedule is likely to go to the mailbox regularly until he finally gets his mail, whereas the other person will go only once. Some behaviors that we refer to as "anxious" (for example, continually checking the mailbox, repeatedly looking out the window to see if a member of the family is coming home, or going to the stove time after time to see if the pot is boiling) result from variable-interval schedules.

Different effects of fixed-interval and variable-interval schedules of reinforcement have been shown dramatically in carefully controlled laboratory studies. It is typical to find that behavior reinforced at *fixed intervals* does not occur regularly. There is a tendency for a pause in responding to occur immediately after each reinforcement, since responses are never reinforced again right after reinforcement has just occurred. This pause in responding is followed by a gradual increase in response rate, which accelerates as the time for the next reinforcement draws near.

This pattern of responding—pauses followed by an increasing response rate—can be eliminated with a *variable-interval* schedule. On this schedule the probability of being reinforced at any given time remains low and constant. Since reinforcement sometimes occurs just after a previous reinforcement, the organism continues to respond at a stable and uniform rate, and the pause noted in fixed-interval schedules tends to disappear. Skinner notes that pigeons operating on a VI schedule with an average interval of five minutes (with food as the reinforcer) have performed for up to 15 hours at a rate of two or three responses per second, pausing no more than 15 to 20 seconds during the entire period of time. Thus, the more random the occurrence of reinforcement, the more constant the response rate is likely to be.

With regard to ratio schedules of reinforcement, the important consideration is "the ratio of reinforced to unreinforced responses." A *fixed-ratio* (FR) schedule requires a specific, constant number of responses for each reinforcement. A *variable-ratio* (VR) schedule requires a varied number of responses for each reinforcement, with the ratios varying around some average number. For example, a rat operating on a *fixed-ratio* schedule may have to press the Skinner box lever 20 times for each pellet of food. If the rat were operating on a *variable-ratio* schedule, the average number of presses would be 20, with the required number being sometimes 2, sometimes 40, 15, 25, and so on.

The following table may help in keeping straight the four basic schedules of intermittent reinforcement.

Schedules of Intermittent Reinforcement			
Interval (Time)		Ratio (Number)	
Fixed (FI)	Variable (VI)	Fixed (FR)	Variable (VR)

An important difference between interval schedules and ratio schedules is that, in the former case, reinforcement is *not* dependent on the amount of behavior, but in the latter case it *does* depend on the amount of behavior.

A classic example of a fixed-ratio schedule is factory piecework. The employee has to produce a certain number of "pieces" in order to be reinforced (paid). Skinner also gives examples such as a student who has to complete a project in order to get a grade and a salesperson who is working on commission. If the number of responses required for reinforcement is not too great, a high response rate is commonly maintained by a fixed-ratio schedule. In plain language, working hard pays off. However, as Skinner points out, fatigue may occur and become a limiting factor.

With fixed-ratio schedules that are in operation for long periods, and especially when the ratios are high, an effect similar to that found with fixed-interval schedules may occur. That is, there may be a pause in responding just after reinforcement. However, in contrast to fixed-interval schedules, once responding begins again on a fixed-ratio schedule, the rate tends to be high immediately; the more gradual acceleration in response rate seen on FI schedules is not typical of FR schedules.

When the number of responses required for the next reinforcement exceeds some limit, responding sometimes stops completely for a considerable length of time; Skinner refers to this condition as *abulia*. An example is the case of a person who works extremely hard to get a college degree and then is unable to begin the difficult task of finding a good job. The reinforcement schedule has "strained" the person. Laboratory studies with pigeons suggest that this "strain" is not physical fatigue but can be considered as a failure to continue performing that is related to a very high fixed-ratio schedule.

Just as the pause after reinforcement with a fixed-interval schedule can be eliminated by a variable-interval schedule, the pauses with a fixed-ratio schedule can be gotten rid of with a variable-ratio schedule. A variable-ratio schedule essentially provides a constant probability of reinforcement for each response. Sometimes successive responses are reinforced; at other times many responses may be made before reinforcement occurs. The result is a high, sustained rate of response. Skinner indicates that pigeons will respond at a rate of five times per second and will keep this up for many hours.

A classic example of human behavior that is maintained at a high rate by a variable-ratio schedule is gambling. Roulette wheels, horse races, slot machines, and so on provide variable-ratio reinforcement: the outcome of any particular bet is unpredictable. Skinner suggests that "the pathological gambler exemplifies the result" of such a schedule. There are many, many other examples of behaviors that are reinforced on a variable-ratio basis: getting to know strangers, hunting and fishing, going to the movies, dining out, playing golf, going to parties, writing letters, cooking, tinkering with broken household appliances, watching television, and so on. These behaviors are sometimes reinforced and sometimes not. We engage in many of them often, time after time, year after year, which shows the extent to which we are controlled by this type of schedule of reinforcement. However, to prevent oversimplification, it must be pointed out that sometimes the behaviors just listed may be explained in ways other than variable-ratio schedules. For example, going to the movies and watching TV may be maintained on a variable-ratio schedule, but they also may be behaviors that allow escape from aversive conditions in everyday life.

The basic types of schedules and the main response characteristics associated with each can be summarized as follows:

Interval Schedules: The overall rate of response is generally low when compared with ratio schedules. The longer the interval, the lower the overall response rate. If the intervals are *fixed,* there is a pause immediately after reinforcement, then a gradual increase in the rate of responding, and then increased acceleration as the time for the next reinforcement approaches. If the intervals are *variable,* the pause is eliminated and more constant responding occurs.

Ratio Schedules: The rate of response is generally high (unless the ratio is too high). If the ratios are *fixed,* typically there is a pause immediately after reinforcement and then an abrupt acceleration to a high response rate. With very high ratios, the pause after reinforcement may be long. A *variable-ratio* schedule tends to eliminate the postreinforcement pause and generally results in a high, sustained response rate.

This discussion of reinforcement schedules could go on and on, and we could get involved in tremendous detail and complexity. In their 1957 book, *Schedules of Reinforcement,* C. B. Ferster and Skinner cover 16 different classes of reinforcement schedules, within which there are numerous individual arrangements. Although space limitations prevent a detailed discussion of these various complicated schedules, a few brief examples can be given. On a *multiple schedule* the reinforcements occur according to two or more independent schedules, which may alternate randomly. A stimulus change signals a change in schedules, and this stimulus (or stimuli) remains in effect as long as the particular schedule is operating. Life, in general, might be considered a multiple schedule. We are faced with various stimulus situations—work, classrooms, parties, various persons, and so on—each of which may demand different kinds of behavior for reinforcement. A *concurrent schedule* consists of two or more independent schedules operating at the same time; reinforcement can be obtained on any of these schedules if the appropriate behavior is emitted. In everyday life, concurrent schedules are usually operating. We can do one of two or more things—play or study, go here or there, see one friend or another— and be reinforced for different behaviors. We also may alternate between the schedules. On a *chained schedule,* behavior in the presence of one stimulus produces a second stimulus, behavior in the presence of the second stimulus produces a third stimulus, and so on, until behavior in the presence of the "final" stimulus produces (at least sometimes) a primary reinforcer. The stimuli in the "chain" serve as conditioned reinforcers as well as discriminative stimuli. A chain begins with the presentation of a discriminative stimulus; an appropriate response in the presence of this stimulus produces a conditioned reinforcer, which also serves as a discriminative stimulus for the next response, and so on. If we trace the sequence of responses leading to eating in a restaurant, we might find the following: in the presence of the discriminative stimulus "dinner time," we look for a restaurant; finding a restaurant reinforces looking for it and also acts as a discriminative stimulus for entering; entering is reinforced by the presence of tables, which are also discriminative stimuli for sitting down; sitting down is reinforced by the appearance of a waiter, who is a discriminative stimulus for ordering; ordering is reinforced by the appearance of food, which is the discriminative stimulus for eating. The ingestion of food provides primary reinforcement and maintains the chain of responses involved in going to the restaurant. We certainly wouldn't continue to repeat the sequence if we never received food. Although somewhat oversimplified (because *all* behaviors and stimuli in the sequence have not been considered), this example illustrates the important role of "chaining" in our lives; much operant behavior occurs in chained sequences.

Chaining also can be applied in training situations. Chains of behavior are conceived of as developing initially in a backward direction (that is, the last response produces an important reinforcer, and responses are built backward from that point to some starting point). Toilet training, for example, may begin by reinforcing (with praise) elimination on the toilet. Next, the child can practice how to remove the required clothing. In further training, he or she can be encouraged to go to the bathroom regularly, and so on. This behavioral sequence can be conditioned by the praise given after the last response in the chain. Something similar to this process probably is what happens in millions of homes, but it sometimes might occur more efficiently with systematic applications of chaining procedures.

Skinner has demonstrated that pigeons can be trained to perform in a variety of ways through the manipulation of schedules. Since the publication of *Schedules of Reinforcement,* a number of studies have shown that human behavior is also susceptible to specifiable conditions of reinforcement. Although the day has not yet arrived when all human behaviors can be explained in detail by referring to reinforcement schedules, Ferster and Skinner have shown that this possibility exists. They clearly have given us a systematic scheme within which a great variety of behaviors can be interpreted.

It is possible to look around and see that many behaviors are dramatically affected by the ways in which reinforcements occur. Various schedules can be operating. At the risk of oversimplifying, we might explain the hard-driving, highly assertive behavior of a rising business executive in a very competitive industry as resulting from a ratio schedule—he or she must produce at a high rate in order to climb rapidly up the executive ladder via promotions. The harder this executive works, the faster the reinforcements occur (ruling out all those environmental factors that we refer to as "bad luck").

Of course, to show that high productivity results from certain schedules of reinforcement does not mean that these schedules are always desirable in a general sense. For example, misuse of these types of schedules may cause employees to "wear themselves out" or to develop "rigid personalities." The latter may result when the behaviors emitted by a person become almost solely job related (because these behaviors are the main sources of reinforcement). Other behaviors (such as enjoying a hobby, talking about current events, or developing athletic skills), which are said to indicate a "well-rounded personality," may be emitted less and less frequently as work behaviors increase. If these other behaviors are not emitted, there is no chance for them to be reinforced; therefore they will not be strengthened. When this happens, we are likely to say "All he (or she) ever thinks about is work" or "That person is really closed-minded." The individual has a relatively limited behavior repertoire due to the contingencies of reinforcement that have been operating in his or her life.

Although the examples just given involve work behaviors, reinforcement schedules also significantly affect our other activities. Consider sexual activity. If a sexual partner has you operating on a fixed-interval schedule, your behavior is likely to be quite different than it would be if the schedule were variable-ratio. Once a fixed-interval schedule is established, such as a pattern involving sexual intercourse once a week on Saturday night, sexual approaches to the partner are likely to occur only on Saturday evenings. In between, there will be few, if any, approaches. For contrast, let's assume that a variable-ratio schedule is operating. Since reinforcement (sexual intercourse) occurs irregularly, and each approach to the partner has some probability of success, seductive attempts will be relatively constant and frequent.

As with most psychological concepts, the application of schedules of reinforcement can be oversimplified and misused if done carelessly. Human behavior *is* complex and subject to many influences. However, careful study of a situation with attention focused on the occurrence of reinforcements can yield enlightening and useful findings.

■   SELF-CONTROL AND CREATIVITY   ■

An extremely interesting question to ask of Skinnerian psychology is "Does an individual have any control at all over his or her own behavior?" In discussing schedules of reinforcement, it seemed that behavior control was exerted by environmental contingencies rather than by the person himself or herself. Is the individual helpless and simply a victim of changes in the environment?

Skinner believes that "self-control" can be explained within the framework of radical behaviorism. In self-control, the person is able to identify the behavior to be controlled (this is one way in which it differs from creativity). Often this behavior has had aversive consequences. Drinking heavily, losing one's temper, being lazy, stealing, driving too fast, eating too much, and so on—these responses may have been punished, or there may be the threat of punishment if they occur. Behavior (self-control) that reduces the probability of such punishable responses will be reinforced (here we are talking about negative reinforcement, which, as explained earlier, also strengthens behavior).

Techniques for self-control vary. Some examples are: (1) engaging in some behavior involving physical restraint, such as keeping your hands in your pockets to avoid nail biting; (2) removing yourself from the situation in which the behavior is likely to occur—for example, walking away from a person who is a stimulus for "losing your temper"; (3) removing "temptation"—for example, throwing away cigarettes, which are the stimuli for smoking; (4) staying away from situations likely to provide stimuli that influence the undesirable behavior—for example, avoiding parties or certain friends in order to stop drinking; (5) doing something else, thereby making it impossible to engage in the behavior that is likely to be punished. These self-control behaviors can be negatively reinforced if they reduce the possibility of being punished. Also, they may be reinforced in other ways. For instance, giving up smoking is negatively reinforced by avoiding possible aversive consequences (heart disease, lung cancer, and so on) but also is positively reinforced by others' praise and by the increased ability to perform various physical activities.

Of course, self-control sometimes fails, and the person continues to smoke, to get drunk, to avoid work, and so on. When this happens, it is common to say that the person is "weak" or has "poor character." However, a radical behaviorist does not accept these *explanatory fictions*. The environment must be analyzed carefully to see why these undesirable behaviors are being maintained; it does no good to look for the answer inside the person.

If undesirable behaviors continue, they are being maintained by positive or negative reinforcement. Human behaviors usually have a variety of consequences, and it is not easy to specify which outcomes will be most effective in controlling behavior. Immediate reinforcement often maintains behaviors that have aversive consequences in the long run. Consider alcoholism. The immediate changes caused by drinking may be positively reinforcing, and negative reinforcement may also occur (that is, perhaps the person can escape from the aversiveness of "facing reality"). Therefore, drinking is often strongly influenced by its immediate reinforcing outcomes. If the consequences of drinking become sufficiently aversive (physical illness, loss of income, and so on), then the person may emit behaviors that we refer to as "self-control." Continued self-control will depend on the reinforcing consequences of giving up drinking as well as on the aversive consequences that develop (for example, if "reality" becomes too hard to face, the individual may start drinking again). It should be noted that the whole emphasis in this discussion is on environmental factors, not on "will power" or other hypothetical "inner strengths."

Overeating is a common problem behavior that is relevant in a discussion of self-control. A number of steps can be taken to control eating. (Don't forget, though, that the *immediate* effects of eating are reinforcing and that this a major problem to be overcome.) (1) Using a graph to plot the daily or weekly progression of weight loss can provide relatively quick reinforcement for small losses—one can "see" the results that are difficult to "feel." (2) Reprimanding oneself, or having one's friend supply reprimands, can provide aversive consequences for snacking or for taking second portions; conversely, self-praise, or the praise of friends, can provide positive reinforcement for eating less. (3) Eating a balanced diet lessens the chance of extreme deprivation and loss of self-control. (4) Avoiding stimuli that promote eating makes it easier to "resist temptations." This approach involves everything from staying away from good restaurants and the pastry counter at the grocery store to keeping fattening foods out of the refrigerator and avoiding social functions at which eating is encouraged. (5) Doing other things is important, especially when the craving for food is strong: go for a walk, go to the movies, call a friend, mow the lawn, and so on. These activities prevent eating, and they also may provide alternative reinforcers. These five suggestions deal with changing the environment, and they do not begin with advice about "being strong." If they result in significant weight loss, then lowered eating behavior is often maintained by positive reinforcers associated with being slimmer (for example, greater social acceptance, more attention from others, and heightened physical abilities).

It should be stated explicitly, in case there are any lingering doubts about Skinner's position on self-control, that he believes that control rests ultimately in variables in the environment and in the individual's reinforcement history, *not* in "personal responsiblity." He suggests that it is unnecessary to assume that any inner force exists. Even when "self-determination" appears to be at work, the real control still resides in environmental conditions and in the past and present experiences of the person; even when an individual's behaviors alter the environment, the environment still influences the person's behaviors. We may escape or avoid aversive conditions by behaving in various ways (thereby "exerting self-control"), but the new conditions produced by these behaviors will affect our subsequent actions.

Next, let's briefly consider "creativity." What happens when someone comes up with a "new" solution to a problem, paints a "unique" picture, "invents" a complicated machine, and so on? These kinds of behaviors are often attributed to "genius," and much credit is given to the person for his or her "insight" or "talent." However, if the person's history of reinforcement and genetic endowment could be taken fully into consideration and if present contingencies of reinforcement could be described in detail, there would be less mystery about creative acts.

Persons who perform creatively are not operating in a vacuum; they often have large repertoires of behaviors resulting from their reinforcement histories. Stimuli in the situations in which creativity emerges usually bear some resemblance, however vague, to previously encountered stimuli associated with reinforcement. In the presence of such stimuli, various responses are likely to be made, and these responses may then be differentially reinforced until "unique" behaviors are shaped up.

Skinner suggests that "mutations" in behavior sometimes result from the accidental occurrence of unusual environmental conditions and may contribute to creativity. For example, an artist or worker to whom the usual equipment, tools, or materials are not available may emit quite novel behaviors. If these behaviors are successful (reinforced), the person may be said to be creative. In much the same way that genetic mutations are selected because of their survival value, behavioral mutations are selected because of their reinforcing consequences.

■ CONSCIOUS PROCESSES ■

Skinner does *not* ignore phenomena that we refer to by terms such as "self-awareness" and "thinking." A common misconception concerning radical behaviorism is that these "conscious processes" are given no attention. Skinner has indicated that these *private* events, which can't be observed directly by others, can be analyzed in a way similar to *public* events.

Just as is true of observable behaviors, the covert behaviors of feeling, thinking, and so on are possible because of genetic endowment, and their *specifics* are determined by environmental factors such as contingencies of reinforcement. Simply because feeling, thinking, and so on are going on "within the skin" does not mean they are of a special nature. They still can be considered as responses (though they are covert) and subjected to a behavioristic analysis.

An important and controversial aspect of Skinner's psychology is his view that it is inappropriate and misleading to consider conscious states as causes of behavior. Simply put, feelings and thoughts are considered to be *effects* (of genetic endowment and individual experiences) rather than *causes* of action. More will be said about this later.

Would each of us know what is "going on inside" if reinforcements were not available for making self-observations? Skinner argues that we wouldn't. In his view, we become self-aware primarily through the effects of other people (whom he calls the "verbal community") who direct us to make self-observations and who then reinforce this behavior. They ask us how we feel, what we're thinking, what we know, and then they provide attention, acceptance, concern, and so on when we respond in appropriate ways. This process, continued over a lifetime, results in a great deal of self-observing behavior, commonly called "conscious activity" by non-Skinnerians.

Skinner points out that the *exteroceptive nervous system* allows us to see, hear, taste, smell, and feel certain things in the world around us and also to make limited observations of our own bodies. Also involved in his analysis of conscious processes are *interoceptive stimuli,* arising from our digestive, respiratory, and circulatory systems, and *proprioceptive stimuli,* arising from the positions and movements of our bodies. These stimuli are private in the sense that only the individual directly experiences them, but other people encourage the labeling and "understanding" of these inner events.

The way our responses to our internal stimuli are conditioned can be important. Consider a case in which parents give immediate attention to (reinforce) the slightest sign of discomfort in their child and make suggestions about "being ill." The child then is likely to interpret (respond to) many private stimuli as indications of sickness, and he or she may eventually become a hypochondriac. Similar private stimuli might not be significant to another person whose minor complaints and small physical changes have been ignored by others.

Skinner points out that our knowledge of ourselves may be quite limited. We are likely to make more precise discriminations among external stimuli than among our own internal stimuli. Consider how difficult it is to explain to a doctor the exact nature of an ache or pain. While other persons have direct access to external stimuli and therefore can help us to make fine discriminations by applying reinforcers in a relatively consistent fashion, this is not the case when the stimuli are internal.

To illustrate further, we learn to label accurately many subtle differences among colors, but among how many different types of "love" or "anger" or "embarrassment" can we discriminate? Skinner has pointed out that it is easier to teach a child the difference between the stimuli "red" and "orange" than it is to teach the difference between one pattern of private stimuli called "diffidence" and another called "embarrassment." Perhaps this is why people so often are confused about their thoughts and feelings and why self-knowledge is so difficult to obtain.

In Skinner's analysis of the types of conscious processes that we speak of as "thinking about the solution to a problem" or "deciding which course of action to take," he rejects suggestions that they are self-generated, autonomous functions of the mind. Individuals, in his view, do not find solutions to problems somewhere within themselves, and they don't autonomously "make up their minds" to do certain things.

Cognitive problem solving, Skinner proposes, involves covert problem-solving behaviors and their consequences and is under the control of environmental conditions. This process has the advantages of speed and privacy; in other words, a sequence of covert behaviors and consequences can occur much more quickly and unobtrusively than in their overt forms. Despite its rapid, private quality, *thinking is behaving* in Skinner's view and can be analyzed as behavior. What we think about (for example, the problem-solving strategies that we consider) is influenced by what we have learned through our own actual experiences and through the instructions and advice of others.

Conscious decisions and choices also are controlled by environmental circumstances. When we do one thing rather than another, we often feel that we are making a rational, conscious decision. Free choice seems to be involved, but Skinner's approach suggests that this is an illusion. When we choose or decide, we are simply behaving—and that behavior is influenced by the situations, behaviors, and behavioral consequences of the past and the present (in other words, past and present contingencies of reinforcement are the critical determinants of what we decide or choose to do).

The behaviors of covert problem solving and decision making obviously occur frequently. From a Skinnerian perspective, this is explained by the concept of reinforcement. Both solving problems and making decisions can result in gaining something positive (positive reinforcement) or in avoiding or escaping something aversive (negative reinforcement). Also, if most of the problem-solving or decision-making process occurs covertly, unobserved by others, the person may be admired and praised (reinforced) for his or her "reasoning ability." In addition, the private nature of the process means that a number of alternative behaviors can be tested without suffering real-world consequences for the wrong moves.

Skinner admits that his account of thinking is not complete at this time, but he adds that an explanation of thought as a function of the mind is no explanation at all. He strongly believes that more progress will be made by investigating the relationships between thinking and environmental events than by focusing on some assumed inner-directed process. Also, if we want to teach people how to reason well, the more we know about the effects of environmental factors, the better that job can be done.

The concept of "rule-governed behavior" should also be mentioned. We don't necessarily have to experience directly the actual consequences of behaviors in order to learn. We can be informed or instructed by others about the consequences of particular behaviors; in this way, our behavior sometimes is "rule-governed" rather than "contingency-shaped" (this latter phrase refers to the effects of the natural contingencies of reinforcement to which we are exposed). Much of what we learn is passed on verbally to us by parents, teachers, work supervisors, colleagues, friends, and so on, based on their experiences. Related to the topic we have just been discussing, an important part of our thinking behavior is controlled by "rules" (that is, instructions, proverbs, advice, suggestions, laws, warnings, and so on) that are communicated orally or in writing.

Following or considering rules is behavior that is conditioned in the same way as other behaviors. If doing as we have heard or read is reinforced (as it often is), this behavior will thereby be strengthened and we will continue to follow or consider such information.

There often is a difference between behavior that is rule-governed and behavior that is contingency-shaped. For example, behavior that results from being told how to operate a machine is not likely to be as smooth and efficient as behavior that is controlled by the actual conditions provided by the machine. In many such situations, behavior is initially controlled by instructions but eventually comes under the control of the real existing conditions.

■   DRIVES AND EMOTIONS   ■

It is commonly suggested that behavior results from some force operating within the individual. Let's consider the term "drive." People are said to eat because of the hunger drive, to have intercourse because of the sexual drive, to try to get ahead on their jobs because of a drive to succeed, and so on. Skinner believes that this is *not* the best way to explain behavior. Using the concept of drive in these ways draws attention away from the actual causes of human behavior, which are to be found primarily in the environment. Skinner would rather use the term "drive" simply to refer to the effects of environmental factors that can change the probability of behavior (for example, conditions of deprivation or satiation and various schedules of reinforcement). To state his main point simply: *the most important causes of behavior are environmental, and it only confuses matters to talk about inner drives.*

Skinner has stated specifically that we should *not* consider drives to be (1) stimuli, (2) physiological states, (3) psychic states, or (4) simple states of strength. (For example, it is misleading to talk about a gambler's "strong drive" to gamble; a high rate of gambling behavior may be the result of a variable-ratio schedule of reinforcement.)

If Skinner's advice were taken seriously, the way we view human behavior would be altered dramatically. It is quite easy to believe that behavior results from internal forces; it is harder to accept the often complex task of looking at the environments in which people function to try to determine what factors in these environments are influencing behavior. Also, this latter approach might lead to the conclusion that, in order to bring about significant changes in behavior, it would be necessary to change the status quo, which can be a very threatening proposal. Rather than considering changes in the environments of schools, industries, prisons, marriages, families, and so on, we often would rather talk about "unmotivated" students and teachers, "lazy" workers, "rebellious" prisoners, "irresponsible" wives and husbands, "unconcerned" fathers and mothers, and "wild and disrespectful" children—as if all these problems were generated by "perverse" internal states.

Let us now briefly consider emotions. Does Skinner deny that we are influenced by our emotional states? Don't we sometimes strike out at others because of "anger"? Don't we sometimes touch and hold another person because of "love"? Don't we sometimes hastily retreat from certain situations because of "fear"? A radical behaviorist's answer to such questions again emphasizes that simply referring to inner states, such as emotions, does not really explain anything. The inner states that we call emotions must themselves be explained, rather than being used to explain behavior. (Skinner himself occasionally talks about emotions, but he is referring to a pattern of internal and external responses and not to inner causes of behavior.)

The problem in a behavioristic analysis of emotion is to determine the environmental conditions that result in "emotional" responses. As in other behavioral analyses, contingencies of reinforcement are important; that is, situations, responses, and behavioral consequences must be considered. Some simple examples follow. In each case, *both* the inner emotional response *and* the overt emotional behavior are explained by referring to environmental events. Also, both respondent and operant conditioning may be involved.

A person may feel angry *and* strike someone because of past and present aversive conditions and negative reinforcement. Perhaps the person struck resembles someone who in the past was annoying or abusive—that is, someone who provided aversive stimuli. Generalization may occur, so that the present person is reacted to similarly to the way the original annoying individual was reacted to (thereby a feeling of anger is aroused). In addition, negative reinforcement for hitting may have occurred in the past: striking annoying or abusive persons may have stopped their aversive behaviors (therefore hitting is likely in the present situation).

Persons who feel love often behave "lovingly" by touching and holding their loved ones. But rather than saying that these behaviors result from the emotion of love, Skinner would suggest that both loving feelings *and* loving behaviors often result from mutual positive reinforcement: shared attention, expressions of approval and affection, sexual contact, and so on are powerful reinforcers, capable of giving rise to the inner responses that we call "love" and of strengthening overt behaviors such as touching and holding.

We'll consider one more situation involving emotion. If someone suddenly starts shouting loudly at us, we may be "startled"; our hearts may beat faster, our muscles may contract, and other physiological reactions may occur. We may label these private, internal stimuli as "fear" (because of past conditioning by the verbal community). Also, we may respond to the situation by moving away quickly (because this response was negatively reinforced in the past—that is, moving away resulted in the termination of aversive stimuli). It is interesting to consider that some persons might, because of different conditioning, label the private stimuli as "anger" and respond to the situation by aggressing against the person doing the shouting. In this type of analysis, the emotions of "fear" and "anger" are explained in behavioristic terms, involving stimuli, responses, and consequences. Both reflexive responses (such as faster heartbeat) and operant behaviors (such as moving away) are involved.

AVERSIVE CONTROL
AND PUNISHMENT

Some issues to be mentioned in this section have already been touched on. However, they are related so importantly to Skinner's psychology that they need to be repeated and expanded upon somewhat.

"Aversive control" is a very popular method for getting people to behave in desired ways. Conditions are arranged so that individuals do what is expected of them in order to escape from or avoid aversive consequences. Governments, churches, schools, industries, and other social institutions often use this method to control the behavior of citizens, members, students, and workers, respectively.

Individuals also control one another's behaviors through aversive measures. A husband may get his wife to be submissive and subservient by controlling her economic condition; if she doesn't behave the way he wants her to, he may refuse to give her money. If she has no independent source of support, this can be a very effective means of control. Controls such as this often operate in very subtle, unspoken ways; the behavior of both persons is controlled by what is going on, but the actual situation may never become obvious. Aversive control also is often characteristic of parent-child relationships. Children may behave "appropriately" to avoid having their allowances or other privileges taken away or in order to stop their parents' constant nagging. Conversely, the parents may sometimes "give in" to a child's demands in order to stop the crying, sulking, pleading, or other behavior that is aversive to them. In this case, it is the child who is using aversive control.

Skinner is opposed to the use of aversive control in human relations or for the purposes of society's institutions. He believes that positive reinforcement is a much more effective means of controlling behavior, mainly because its outcomes are more predictable and because it is less likely to generate undesirable behaviors. As an example of the possible ill effects of aversive control, consider students who react to teachers' threats (designed to promote studying) by staying out of school, drop-ping out completely, committing acts of vandalism, or becoming apa-thetic and uncaring. Skinner suggests that such behaviors are inevi-table outcomes of aversive control.

Punishment is no good either, according to Skinner. He has been firmly against its use for many years. Whereas *aversive control* is intended to promote expected behaviors, *punishment* is intended to suppress unwanted behaviors. In his 1948 novel, *Walden Two*, Skin-ner argued vehemently that punishment is an evil, and he has contin-ued that line of thought in various subsequent writings. He claims that punishment (presenting an aversive stimulus after a response or removing a positive reinforcer after a response) is not the opposite of reinforcement. It does not weaken the overall tendency to respond, although it may *temporarily* suppress certain behaviors. As with aver-sive control, punishment often has undesirable outcomes.[7] For exam-ple, (1) situations similar to those in which punishment has occurred may be avoided, as when a punished student stays away from all learn-ing situations; (2) the punished person's "bad" behavior may be sup-pressed *only* in the presence of the punisher; (3) if punishment occurs intermittently, there may be a conflict between the tendency to emit the response and the tendency to hold it back (this kind of conflict may be seen in the behavior of persons referred to as "indecisive" or "unsure of themselves"); (4) if no alternatives to the punished behavior are avail-able, the person may become "unresponsive" and "withdrawn."

If punishment is a poor technique, what other methods can be used to get rid of undesirable behaviors? (1) *The circumstances that result in unwanted behaviors sometimes can be modified.* Cheating on exams can be reduced by giving open-book or take-home exams, by changing the emphasis on grades, or by arranging the situation so that it is not possible to cheat. Another problem behavior, stealing, would be greatly reduced if the economic system provided sufficiently for everyone. Aggressiveness can usually be decreased by reducing "frustrating" ele-ments in the environment. These kinds of examples could go on and on. (2) *Unwanted behaviors sometimes can be ignored and thereby extinguished.* If reinforcement (such as "attracting attention") doesn't occur, behavior tends to diminish in frequency. One major problem with extinction is that it is sometimes a lengthy process. Another prob-lem is that "emotional" outbursts may result when reinforcement is withheld; responses commonly referred to as "anger" or "frustration" may occur. These responses can be very aversive, and it is sometimes difficult to continue ignoring such behavior. (3) *Incompatible behav-*

---

[7]Strong punishment may *permanently* suppress behaviors, but it may also cause extreme "emotional" reactions and responses that seriously hinder further learning. Whenever punishment is used, there is the chance of creating "emotional by-products."

iors sometimes can be conditioned. For example, if a child is very aggressive and continually makes loud demands of others, changes might be brought about by ignoring (extinguishing) these aggressive behaviors and giving attention and approval (positive reinforcement) for quieter, more cooperative behaviors. Using this technique may get results faster than using extinction by itself.

Alternatives to aversive control and punishment *are* available. Why aren't these alternatives used more often? Probably because they some-times are more difficult to implement and may take some time before they are effective. The easy and quick way to control others' behavior is to use threats or to punish; all that is required to use these methods is power. In the long run, however, they may backfire.

■ PROBLEM BEHAVIOR:
CAUSES AND REMEDIES ■

Skinner has suggested that the explanations for neurotic, psychotic, and other problem behaviors often may be found in environmental fac-tors such as unique histories of reinforcement, conditions of extreme deprivation or satiation, intense aversive control, and harsh punish-ment. It is likely that the same basic explanatory concepts apply to both "normal" and "abnormal" behaviors (except that in the latter case the effects of environmental factors are more dramatic). The troublesome or dangerous behaviors that are often considered to reflect "mental illness" may simply be *learned.*

The extremely emotional behaviors that characterize phobias can be used as an illustration. A sudden, dramatic change in behavior can be observed when the phobic individual encounters certain situations or when certain internal events occur, as when he or she thinks about a particular situation. Rapid heartbeat, sweating, blanching, and other conditioned reflexive responses may be seen, as well as operant behav-iors such as escape or avoidance responses. The question is "Why does the person have these reactions?" To say "He (or she) has a phobia" or "He (or she) has an emotional conflict" or "He (or she) has an uncon-scious fear" may get us off on the wrong foot in looking for the answers and in making suggestions for treatment. It might be more productive, as Skinner suggests, to consider these behaviors as *learned* responses (for example, the result of the punishing consequences of some past behavior in a particular situation) and then to set out to change them directly, without attempting to analyze some "inner emotional prob-lem." According to this view, *the problem is in the behavior, not in the person.*

Someone might ask "Well, what about the panicky thoughts and feel-ings that this fearful person has? Don't they exist *within* him (or her)? How do you deal with *them?*" It must constantly be remembered that

Skinner does not differentiate between the basic nature of events "within the skin" and events in the outside environment. Whatever occurs, occurs in a world of stimuli, responses, and consequences. An individual's thoughts and feelings are responses that can be conditioned and affected by stimuli and consequences, just as overt responses are. Many conditions affect *both* overt and covert responses; punishment and aversive control may result in emotional responses that anyone can see (such as overt escape and avoidance behaviors) as well as responses that only the individual directly experiences (such as particular "feelings" and "thoughts"). The fact that some events are *public* and others are *private* does not necessarily make them subject to different principles—the explanations for both may well be the same.

As indicated earlier, much problem behavior can be traced to excessive aversive control or punishment. To escape, individuals may physically withdraw or run away, or they may do so through behaviors that are less easily observed, such as hallucinating, daydreaming, not paying attention, and so on. Violent counteraggression against the controlling forces may occur; if there is no opportunity for this response, extreme passivity may be an alternative way of avoiding aversive control.

Since various stimuli are present when a person is subjected to aversive control or punishment, these stimuli (through respondent conditioning) may later elicit the same emotional reactions of fear, anxiety, depression, anger, and so on that were elicited in the original situation. This process accounts for many of our "irrational" reactions. If a child is severely punished in school for not studying, various emotional responses will be aroused in the presence of school stimuli. These same responses—fear, anxiety, and so on—may then occur whenever the child is in school or when he or she attempts to study. If other conditioning does not occur and if the emotional reactions do not extinguish, the child may eventually drop out of school and perhaps avoid educational situations for the rest of his or her life. Obviously, this could have far-ranging effects on the person. More extreme punishment might have even stronger effects; such intense fear, anxiety, or other reactions might occur that the person would be considered "very neurotic" or "psychotic." Of course, seldom does a single occurrence in one's life have these dramatic effects. However, think about the possible effects of repeated punishments and attempts at aversive control, applied year after year.

Problem behaviors can result from factors other than aversive control or punishment, such as inadequate positive reinforcement and reinforcement for inappropriate behaviors. For example, in a crowded home or school situation the parent or teacher may be too busy to pay attention to a child who is behaving well. This neglect may not be important if the child's good behavior is being reinforced in other ways, such as by peer approval and attention or through activities that can be engaged in alone. However, suppose these positive reinforcers don't exist; for example, if a student is to be reinforced by reading, writing, drawing, doing math, and other activities that can be done alone, he or she must first have learned to do them. These activities are not reinforcing in and of themselves unless some level of proficiency is reached or unless progress is being made (that is, the student must be effectively manipulating his or her environment).

If a child is being ignored when he or she is behaving well and good behavior is not being reinforced in other ways, there will be a tendency to develop a repertoire of behaviors that *do* get reinforced. Dramatic behaviors often get attention: crying, complaining, screaming, hitting, tardiness, truancy, vandalism, and so on. These behaviors may be shaped up and maintained by the attention they receive, even when the attention consists of reprimands and threats (*any* type of attention may be better than *no* attention). Children who behave in these ways are often given some label such as "extremely disruptive" or "emotionally disturbed," and the existing contingencies of reinforcement are ignored. When this happens, an *explanatory fiction* is being invoked.

Behavior that is dangerous or troublesome to the individual or to society may require treatment. Skinner suggests that therapy should focus on changing observable behaviors and conditions, not on detecting some inner mental or emotional problem. His assumption is that troubling thoughts or feelings will improve when external behaviors and conditions are improved. An analysis of the contingencies of reinforcement in the person's life often indicates what needs to be changed. This involves evaluating the situations to which the person is exposed, the specific ways in which he or she behaves in those situations, and the resulting consequences. Once these details are known, the person can be helped to change conditions that he or she finds aversive, to shape up and maintain more constructive behaviors, and to extinguish unwanted behaviors.

Psychologists and other professionals who apply Skinnerian concepts in treating problem behaviors are usually called "behavior modifiers," and their approaches are called "behavior-modification" procedures. Unlike many psychotherapists, they do not try to change something inside the person, such as a "weak ego" or a "distorted self-concept." They believe that success lies in finding and manipulating the conditions that produce and maintain problem behaviors, and their methods are being used with increasing frequency in a wide variety of situations. (The fundamentals of these methods also can be taught relatively quickly to parents, teachers, and others.) A first step in a behavior-modification program is to describe precisely the behaviors of concern, so that there is an objective and specific account of what needs changing. Then, as attempts are made to alter these behaviors, changes are monitored closely to assess the amount of progress being made.

Some brief examples may help clarify the application of certain behavior-modification procedures. A child who behaves in withdrawn, antisocial ways may be "brought out" if such behaviors are ignored (extinguished) while attention (reinforcement) is given for any minor social acts. Next, increasing sociability would be required to maintain attention. (This is "shaping," a process that was discussed earlier.) Overly aggressive behavior sometimes can be dealt with by ignoring tantrums and other disruptive behaviors (if they are not so intense that the child or someone else may be injured) and by giving attention and approval for nonaggressive, cooperative behaviors. In mental hospitals, bizarre behaviors of psychotic patients sometimes change when such actions no longer are reinforced (when they do not result in attention from nurses, attendants, and so on) and when alternative, "normal" behaviors do bring reinforcement. Autistic, nonverbal children and catatonic, mute adults have been treated effectively with shaping techniques; at first, any attention given to the "teacher" is reinforced (for example, with a treat such as gum, candy, or soda), then any sound, then closer and closer approximations to words, then responses to questions, and so on, until the person initiates speech.

A system used to change behaviors in various settings (including mental hospitals, schools, and homes for juvenile delinquents) is the *token economy.* "Tokens" (which may be in the form of poker chips, play money, and so on) are conditioned reinforcers; once earned, they can be exchanged for food, privileges, or other basic reinforcers. To earn tokens, individuals have to perform some specified behavior: a mental-hospital patient may have to clean up his or her room; a student may have to complete a homework assignment; a delinquent may have to refrain from fighting and attend classes regularly. Although generalization of the positive behaviors beyond the token-economy system is not always assured, this is a desirable possibility. In some cases the outcomes of the behaviors themselves become reinforcing, and therefore the token system can be faded out. For example, the patient's cleaning may be reinforced by more tidy surroundings, the student's studying may be reinforced by what he or she is learning, and the delinquent's improved behaviors may be reinforced by new friendships and accomplishments.

Skinner has provided an interesting analysis of why some traditional psychotherapists are effective in dealing with certain problem behaviors: they provide a "nonpunishing audience." In receptive and uncritical therapy situations, patients begin to emit behaviors that have been suppressed in other situations because of punishment or threatened punishment. Forgotten experiences may be recalled, aggression may be displayed, and there may be illogical behaviors. Some of the effects of punishment extinguish when previously punished behaviors occur in the presence of the nonpunishing therapist. In other words, the "emotional" reactions generated by these behaviors decrease. The patient feels less guilty, sinful, and so on and also is less likely to engage in escape or avoidance behaviors.

It should be mentioned that Skinner does not deny the possibility that some neurophysiological disorders (such as brain damage) can result in problem behaviors. He does, however, continually emphasize the importance of environmental determinants and feels that these factors should always be carefully analyzed to avoid jumping to premature conclusions about other causes.

As well as being applicable to more serious "abnormal" or troublesome behaviors, Skinner's concepts can be applied to common personal behavioral problems in everyday life. Most of us would like to "improve ourselves" in some way or other. For example, we may feel that it would be better to be more pleasant to others. To bring about this modification of behavior, we could keep a week-long record of the number of times we say something pleasant to someone else (simply seeing these data is sometimes sufficient to cause a behavior change); this record gives a "baseline" with which to compare later frequencies of behavior. We can then set a goal to increase slightly the number of pleasant remarks; this goal should be reasonable enough to allow success (reinforcement) to occur. To help achieve this goal, some enjoyable (reinforcing) activity that we perform regularly—having an extra cup of coffee, going to the movies, playing golf, or whatever—should be made contingent on saying something nice to another person. In other words, a positive reinforcer is made to occur after the desired behavior is emitted.

Once the established goal is reached, then a new goal involving a higher response frequency can be set. Sometimes a point system (similar to a token economy) helps; each pleasant comment may be counted as a point, and a certain number of points must then be earned before we reinforce our improved behavior by engaging in the enjoyable activity. The number of points required can be gradually increased. (For an example similar to this, and for many other suggestions about modifying one's own behavior, see D. L. Watson and R. G. Tharp's *Self-Directed Behavior: Self-Modification for Personal Adjustment*, 4th ed., Brooks/Cole, 1985.) An important aspect of "self-improvements" is that they are often maintained by their own reinforcing consequences; for example, other people are likely to react in "nicer" (more reinforcing) ways when we are more pleasant to them.

During recent years, Skinner has become increasingly concerned with the problems associated with growing old. As expected, he approaches these problems from his behavioral perspective, emphasizing practical techniques that can be used to cope with the physical and intellectual limitations that result from aging. To remember to bring your umbrella, hang it on the doorknob when the weather forecast predicts rain; to remember good ideas, keep a notepad or tape recorder handy; to avoid forgetting what you were going to say while talking with someone, speak in shorter and simpler sentences; to be intellectually productive, work fewer hours per day and avoid taxing leisure-time activities such as chess or complicated puzzles (it's better to do nonintellectual things when relaxing); and to lessen the fear of death, avoid continually talking about it, spend more time with younger people who are absorbed in life rather than death, and try to get involved in interesting activities (his point is that, if more time is spent enjoyably, less time will be spent fearing death).[8] These are just a few of Skinner's suggestions for more successful aging. (For more suggestions, see the references relating to aging that are listed at the end of this chapter.)

■ **COMMENTARY** ■

Skinner's radical behaviorism isn't the only form of behaviorism that exists today, but it has attracted the most attention. One reason is that it is a strong, dramatically stated challenge to our traditional ways of explaining human behavior. As detailed earlier, Skinner doesn't allow inner states, such as feelings and thoughts, to enter into his explanations of observable behaviors. While acknowledging that feelings and thoughts exist, he doesn't consider them to be *causes* of our actions. In his view, they can be analyzed as *effects:* genetic endowment supplies the neurophysiological means to feel and think, while individual environmental histories and current circumstances determine the details of feelings and thoughts.

Skinner analyzes feelings, thoughts, and other inner events in essentially the same way as overt behaviors such as reading aloud, writing, driving a car, or throwing a ball. Whether an event is internal and publicly unobservable, or external and publicly observable, the crucial factors are genetic endowment and most specifically, environmental experiences of the individual.

This brings us again to the controversial Skinnerian perspective: feelings and thoughts don't cause our behaviors; rather, they too are responses to be explained. This contradicts much that we have learned as members of a society in which there is a heavy reliance on inner

[8]In an article by Alfie Kohn in *Boston Magazine* ("B. F. Skinner: Reinforced by Life," July 1984, pp. 100–101, 130, 132), Skinner is quoted as saying that he doesn't fear death but does fear not finishing his work. He also remarked that, when he no longer enjoys life, he is not going to stay around. Despite an operation for cancer and such problems of aging as failing eyesight and hearing, Skinner has managed to remain active and productive.

states—happiness, joy, hope, courage, depression, anxiety, sadness, anger, and so on—when explaining overt behavior.

To repeat a very important point made earlier, Skinner would have us avoid the mistake of continually using states of mind or emotion as "explanatory fictions." For example, behavior is often attributed to feelings in statements such as "He didn't go to work today because he felt discouraged" or "I worked hard today because I felt good." In a Skinnerian analysis, however, it might be found that a lack of positive reinforcement on the job causes an employee to stay home from work *and* to feel discouraged, while working hard *and* feeling good can result from the presence of positive reinforcement. In other words, feelings and states of mind are collateral or accompanying products of the same environmental factors (for example, contingencies of reinforcement) that affect overt behaviors.

Is it really important to avoid using feelings and states of mind as explanations of behavior? What harm does it do? The answer to these questions, from Skinner's perspective, is that it has led us astray in our attempts to deal with personal and social problems. We focus too much on internal conditions that cannot be observed and changed directly and pay too little attention to environmental factors that *can* be directly observed and altered. In simple terms, we are wasting our time when we do not go immediately to the source of our problems.

Skinner believes that analyzing and changing *contingencies of reinforcement* (that is, the situations in which behavior occurs, the behavior itself, and the consequences of behavior) provide the key to better individual and social functioning. Attempting to analyze and change inner states is, at best, an indirect and inefficient route; in Skinner's view, in one way or another, sooner or later, external conditions have to be changed if overt behaviors *and* feelings, thoughts, decisions, plans, motives, and so on are to improve.

To Skinner, there is no mystery as to why feelings and other inner states often are relied on to explain behavior. For one thing, they are immediate; that is, they frequently accompany overt behavior and are experienced "first-hand." For example, if we write a letter of complaint to a store from which we have bought a defective product, we are likely to feel annoyed as we write the letter. If asked why we are writing the letter, the most immediate reason seems to be our annoyance. However, both the letter writing and the annoyance actually are caused by objective, environmental circumstances. Because of their intensity, stronger inner responses, such as anger, hatred, love, joy, or acute anxiety, are especially likely to be stated as causes for action.

Another reason why inner states are so often used to explain behavior is that environmental explanations frequently are very difficult to construct. A complex, very subtle, or long-past set of conditions may be determining a person's feelings and overt behaviors in a current situation. Given the difficulties of finding the critical environmental factors, the feelings become the explanation used.

By suggesting that inner states are not causal factors, Skinner by no means belittles their importance. In fact, he encourages the widespread use of positive reinforcement, which he believes produces good feelings. He contrasts this approach with the unpleasant feelings produced in those whose behavior is controlled through negative reinforcement or punishment. Also, the methods of education that he proposes are designed to improve the covert behavior of thinking, as well as overt skills and performance. The implication of Skinner's approach is that better feelings, thoughts, and other inner states result from better external conditions.

Along with his challenge to traditional ways of considering inner states, Skinner has suggested that our concepts of "freedom" and "dignity" are also outdated. In fact, they involve behaviors that hinder the development of a better-functioning society. In his book *Beyond Freedom and Dignity* (1971), he explains that attempts to escape or avoid control in *any* form prevent the widespread use of behavioral technology. In his view, we are so concerned about preserving our freedom and dignity that we ignore the major advances, both individual and societal, that could be brought about through systematic, broadly applied behavior-management techniques (which are based on the concept of positive reinforcement).

While agreeing that we should be free from aversive controlling measures, such as threats of punishment, Skinner suggests that it is dangerous to label all control as bad. Also, if dignity or worth is given to individuals only when it seems that they have behaved autonomously, there will be a reluctance to use behavioral technology as a means of furthering human achievements. He believes that these are critical issues and that our survival may depend on whether or not we design a culture in which more desirable and constructive behaviors are shaped and maintained.

Skinner's assumption is that in one way or another our behaviors *are* controlled but that the greatest benefits are derived individually and socially (and the most freedom is felt) when control consists of systematic positive reinforcement. He has mentioned that he himself has been fortunate because so much of his behavior (for example, his research and writing) has been positively reinforced; therefore he feels free, even though he assumes that his behaviors (as well as everyone else's) are completely the result of genetic endowment and environmental conditions.

There are at least two levels at which Skinnerian psychology can be considered. We have just discussed some issues that are related to one level, which has to do with larger, more "molar" applications of Skinner's approach. At this level, the greatest amount of controversy exists. His challenges to long-established concepts of the causal role of inner states and of freedom and dignity have drawn much harsh criticism. The issues that he has raised at this level are likely to be debated with fervor for quite some time.

At another, more "molecular" level, the behavioral approach consists of a number of concepts and procedures that have many practical uses. Luckily, Skinner's ideas at the molar level do not have to be accepted completely before behavioral concepts and procedures can be applied at the more molecular level. Positive reinforcement, extinction, schedules of reinforcement, shaping, contingencies of reinforcement, and so on provide a basis for analyzing, controlling, and improving behavior. There are increasing applications in settings such as institutions and hospitals, businesses and industries, schools and colleges, familes, individual therapy situations, and self-control programs, with results that frequently are impressive.

The concept of "rule-governed behavior," which often is overlooked in discussions of Skinnerian psychology, adds to the practical applicability of radical behaviorism. It points to the fact that behavior can be affected by advice, warnings, suggestions, instructions, laws, and so on. These "rules" generally refer to contingencies of reinforcement; that is, they indicate the probable consequences of certain responses in particular situations. Clearly expressed rules that accurately convey real-world contingencies are important in therapy, education, business, government, and, in fact, all situations in which persons interact verbally.

As important as some "rules" are, they may not be followed. For example, Skinner sees serious difficulties facing those who are attempting to alleviate critical world problems by advising or warning others that certain current practices are likely to destroy us. Socially harmful actions such as polluting the environment, building nuclear weapons, and overpopulating the earth often are immediately and powerfully reinforcing to those who are benefiting from them, and the dangerous long-range consequences are more remote, with less impact. Also, there is a tendency to avoid or ignore those who are sounding warnings, since the warnings are aversive stimuli.

Skinner is not optimistic about the future of the world, saying that it "may be fatally ill."[9] This opinion is a quite recent one for him. Although he is optimistic about changing the behavior of individuals if the relevant environmental variables can be controlled, the relevant variables

---

[9]See Kathleen Fisher's article "World's Prognosis Grim," *APA Monitor*, October 1982, p. 25. Included are a number of quotes from Skinner.

may be out of reach in the cases of some of our most pressing social problems. The most influential persons and institutions may be responding to factors that are difficult or impossible to alter. The best chance seems to be that political, industrial, and religious leaders eventually will be governed by the advice and warnings being offered. How, or if, that will come about is uncertain. Perhaps, Skinner suggests, the young can be educated to become more responsive leaders.

■ REFERENCES FOR CHAPTER 3 ■

Primary Sources (Skinner's Own Writings)

1. *The Behavior of Organisms.* New York: Appleton-Century-Crofts, 1938.
2. *Walden Two.* New York: Macmillan, 1948. (Paperbound.)
3. *Science and Human Behavior.* New York: Macmillan, 1953. (Also in paperbound edition by The Free Press.)
4. Teaching machines. *Scientific American,* November 1961, pp. 90–102.
5. Behaviorism at fifty. *Science,* May 31, 1963, pp. 951–958.
6. Autobiography. In E. G. Boring & G. Lindzey (Eds.), *A History of Psychology in Autobiography.* Vol. 5. New York: Appleton-Century-Crofts, 1967. Pp. 385–413.
7. *The Technology of Teaching.* New York: Appleton-Century-Crofts, 1968. (Paperbound.)
8. *Contingencies of Reinforcement: A Theoretical Analysis.* New York: Appleton-Century-Crofts, 1969.
9. The machine that is man. *Psychology Today,* April 1969, pp. 20–25, 60–63.
10. *Beyond Freedom and Dignity.* New York: Knopf, 1971. (Also in paperbound edition by Bantam/Vintage.)
11. *Cumulative Record: A Selection of Papers.* (3rd ed.) New York: Appleton-Century-Crofts, 1972.
12. *About Behaviorism.* New York: Knopf, 1974. (Paperbound.)
13. *Particulars of My Life.* New York: Knopf, 1976. This is the first volume of Skinner's autobiography. The other two volumes are *The Shaping of a Behaviorist* (1979) and *A Matter of Consequences* (1983), also published by Knopf. (All three books also are available in paperbound editions from New York University Press.)
14. *Reflections on Behaviorism and Society.* Englewood Cliffs, N.J.: Prentice-Hall, 1978.
15. *Enjoy Old Age: Living Fully in Your Later Years.* New York: Norton, 1983. (Also in paperbound edition by Warner Books.) The coauthor is M. E. Vaughan.
16. Intellectual self-management in old age. *American Psychologist,* Vol. 38, No. 3, March 1983, pp. 239–244.
17. Origins of a behaviorist. *Psychology Today,* September 1983, pp. 22–33.
18. The shame of American education. *American Psychologist,* Vol. 39, No. 9, September 1984, pp. 947–954.

Secondary Sources

1. Bower, Gordon H., & Hilgard, Ernest R. *Theories of Learning* (5th ed.). Englewood Cliffs, N.J.: Prentice-Hall, 1981. Pp. 169–211.
2. Evans, Richard I. *B. F. Skinner: The Man and His Ideas.* New York: Dutton, 1968. (Paperbound.)
3. Hall, Calvin S., & Lindzey, Gardner. *Theories of Personality.* (3rd ed.) New York: Wiley, 1978. Chapter 16, pp. 637–680.
4. Hall, Elizabeth. Will success spoil B. F. Skinner? *Psychology Today,* November 1972, pp. 65–72, 130.
5. Hall, Mary Harrington. An interview with "Mr. Behaviorist"—B. F. Skinner. *Psychology Today.* September 1967, pp. 21–23, 68–71.
6. Langone, John. B. F. Skinner: Beyond reward and punishment. *Discover,* September 1983, pp. 38–46.
7. Nye, Robert D. *What Is B. F. Skinner Really Saying?* Englewood Cliffs, N.J.: Prentice-Hall, 1979. (Paperbound.)

Carl Rogers
and
Humanistic
Phenomenology

■ BIOGRAPHICAL SKETCH OF ROGERS ■

Carl R. Rogers was born January 8, 1902, in Oak Park, a suburb of Chicago. His father was a contractor and civil engineer. Both his parents were religiously oriented, although his mother was the more firmly fundamentalist in her views. The family was closely knit, and Rogers indicates that his parents were "devoted and loving," very practical, and "down to earth." There were six children altogether, five of whom were boys.

When Rogers was 12, his parents bought a farm 30 miles from Chicago. During his high school years, he was expected to take responsibility for chores and other farm work. His school grades were very good, and in 1919 he entered the University of Chicago. There he took part in many activities, including a trip to China as a delegate to a World Student Christian Federation Conference. He also developed a duodenal ulcer, which forced him out of college for a time. He received his degree in history in 1924, having taken only one psychology course, and that same year he married. (Rogers has a son and a daughter; his wife died in 1979.)

Next he entered Union Theological Seminary in New York. Although he found his studies there to be very stimulating, he began to realize that he didn't want to be tied to a specific religious doctrine. Eventually he transferred to Teachers College, Columbia University, to work in clinical and educational psychology. He received his Ph.D. from this institution in 1931.

In 1928, before receiving his doctorate, he began working in Rochester, New York, primarily with delinquent and underprivileged children referred by courts and agencies to the Child Study Department. During 1939–1940 he was director of the Rochester Guidance Center. In 1940 he went to Ohio State University as a professor, and from 1945 until 1957 he was associated with the Counseling Center at the University of Chicago. He then moved on to the University of Wisconsin as a professor. In 1964 he joined the Western Behavioral Sciences Institute as a resident fellow. Since 1968 he has been a resident fellow at the Center for Studies of the Person in La Jolla, California.

Some of Rogers' books are *Counseling and Psychotherapy* (1942), *Client-Centered Therapy* (1951), *On Becoming a Person* (1961), *Carl Rogers on Encounter Groups* (1970), *Becoming Partners: Marriage and Its Alternatives* (1972), *Carl Rogers on Personal Power* (1977), *A Way of Being* (1980), and *Freedom to Learn for the 80's* (1983).

■ HUMANISTIC PHENOMENOLOGY ■

Rogers' view of humans is generally referred to as a "self theory," a "phenomenological theory," or an "actualization theory." Each of these labels emphasizes some important aspect of his thinking. The phrase "humanistic phenomenology" isn't commonly used. However, in my opinion, it is quite appropriate for summing up Rogers' position.

According to Abraham Maslow, the well-known former professor at Brandeis University, humanistic psychology constitutes a "third force" in American psychology, the other two forces being psychoanalysis and behaviorism. Rogers can be considered part of this "third force." Like Maslow, he sees humans as having a natural tendency toward *actualization*. (Although "actualization" is not identical in Maslow's and Rogers' theories, in both cases it includes the growth and fulfillment of basic potentialities. Humans are viewed as essentially growth oriented, forward moving, and concerned with existential choices.) Rogers assumes that basic human nature is positive—that there is nothing inherently negative or evil about us. He suggests that, if we are not forced into socially constructed molds, but rather are accepted for what we are, we will live in ways that enhance both ourselves *and* society. According to Rogers, humans basically need and want both personal fulfillment and close, intimate relationships with others. All in all, it certainly seems that his perspective is a humanistic one.

How does phenomenology fit in? Phenomenology stresses the importance of the individual's immediate conscious experiences in determining reality, and Rogers maintains that knowledge of these individual perceptions of reality is required for the understanding of human behavior. He suggests that each of us behaves in accordance with our subjective awareness of ourselves and of the world around us. The implication is that objective reality (whatever that might be) is *not* the important determinant of our actions; rather, we react on the basis of how we view that reality. Some people try to test very carefully their subjective assumptions about reality by considering as many sources of information as possible (for example, various sensory data, other persons' opinions, and the results of scientific studies), whereas others are less attuned to possibly conflicting information and hold more rigidly to particular perspectives.

There is no one sure path to a "true reality" by which to live, but Rogers believes that openness and responsiveness to all information-gathering possibilities will generally keep the individual going in a satisfactory direction toward increasing growth and fulfillment (actualization). The person must be open and responsive to inner experiencing (sensations, feelings, thoughts, and so on) as well as to the external environment. Humans, according to Rogers, do not know their full potential. They are in a state of "being and becoming," and it is inappropriate at the present time to establish *absolute* criteria about the level of actualization that can be achieved. Everything possible should be done to promote an atmosphere in which humans can continue to expand themselves personally and socially, but the long-range outcomes of the unfolding of human development are beyond the realm of present knowledge.

In both his therapeutic and his research work, Rogers has used a phenomenological approach in his attempts to understand human behavior. He has tried to unravel the difficulties of perceiving reality through another person's eyes. Of special importance are his efforts to understand how individuals view themselves—that is, the assumptions they make about who and what they are and about the nature of their relationships with others.

A few simple examples may clarify further the importance of considering an individual's view of reality when attempting to understand his or her behavior. One person might perceive a large approaching dog as something to be feared, whereas another person might see the same dog as neutral or friendly. As a result, the behaviors of these two individuals in response to the dog are likely to be different. Similarly, the behaviors of each of three persons undergoing a job change will be different if one sees the change as a challenge, another views it as a threat to security, and the third perceives it as an annoyance. The way each of us perceives the reality of *ourselves* is also extremely important. Persons who think of themselves as having little worth and who don't trust their own decision-making power are bound to behave differently from those who feel that they *are* worthy and who *are* confident of their ability to make choices about their lives.

In brief, then, referring to Rogers' theory of personality as "human-istic pheomenology" calls attention to his respect for human beings as individuals who have, as their most basic nature, a tendency to strive for growth and fulfillment and who must be understood in terms of their particular conceptualizations of reality. Rogers is fundamentally an optimist about human potential. He feels that, if people are freed from restricting, corrupting social influences, they can achieve a high level of personal *and* interpersonal functioning and can avoid the real-ity distortions that prevent the achievement of ever-greater growth and fulfillment (actualization).

■ DETERMINISM PLUS FREEDOM ■

⚹The issue of *determinism* (the view that behavior is determined by various factors outside the person's control) versus *freedom* (the view that behavior is a function of personal choice or free will) is rather complex in Rogers' thinking. He advocates a position that acknowl-edges both of these possibilities. He states that determinism "is the foundation stone of present-day science" (Rogers, 1983, p. 295) and that, as a scientist, he can accept the fact that behavior is absolutely determined. He believes that valuable information can be gathered by studying the objective factors that influence human behavior; however, he goes on to suggest that this information is used most productively *only* when it is combined with data from other sources—namely, from one's own subjective experiencing and from the empathic understand-ing of others. In other words, objective scientific inquiry (based on deterministic assumptions) has a place in the study of humans, but this approach is limited because it leaves out something: *inner human experiencing* (that is, the totality of inner sensations, thoughts, feel-ings, perceptions, memories, and so on). To understand this experi-encing more fully, persons must subjectively evaluate themselves and attempt to gain empathic understanding (phenomenological knowl-edge) of the experiencing of others.

As a scientist Rogers recognizes the usefulness of a deterministic view. As a therapist his emphasis is different. He has seen the utility of conceiving of humans in the therapeutic relationship as having free-dom of choice based on an openness and responsiveness to the totality of their experiencing. He suggests that, as therapy progresses, individ-uals become more and more able to make decisions and to choose to act on these decisions. He believes that his clients (Rogers prefers to use the term "client" rather than "patient") develop toward freedom as they become less defensive and less distorted in their reactions to their total inner experiencing and their social and physical environments. Maladjusted persons, according to Rogers, are less free; their behavior is patterned more rigidly; they are relatively incapable of exerting free choice and often feel uncomfortably inhibited or restricted. This is because they are denying or distorting their inner experiencing as well as their environmental circumstances.

Rogers believes that, when persons are functioning well, they experience a feeling of considerable freedom. Such individuals also *behave* as if they were free. It can be said that they *choose* to act in effective ways, consistent with all the internal and external stimuli that are present. However, from a different perspective it can be said that their behavior is *determined* by all the existing factors, since certain behaviors *will* be more satisfying than others. Rogers seems to mean that, at the same time the individual chooses, his or her behavior is being determined by all the relevant conditions that exist. The open, responsive person is fully aware of all that is going on inside and also has an accurate picture of existing external factors. This individual is free, but he or she *will* take a particular course of action; in the presence of all available stimuli there are definitely certain behaviors that are most productive from *both* subjective and objective points of view. In this case there isn't any contradiction between free will and determinism—in a sense, they coincide.

If this discussion seems labored, take heart; Rogers himself admits that he has been "perplexed" about the paradox that exists between determinism and freedom. One of his most important thoughts on the matter is that *both* assumptions are important. In his view, *determinism* serves a vital function in scientific analyses of behavior, and the notion of *freedom* is critical for effective personal and interpersonal functioning (for example, in therapeutic relationships).

■ SOURCES OF DATA ■

Rogers' ideas developed mainly in the context of client-centered therapeutic relationships. A word must be said at this point regarding this type of therapy, which originated with Rogers. (The subject will be discussed in greater detail in a later section of this chapter.) The term "client" is used because it emphasizes the person's active, voluntary, and responsible participation; also, it suggests equality between the therapist and the person seeking help, avoiding the implication that the individual is sick or that he or she is being experimented upon.

The focus in client-centered therapy is on the clients' efforts to come to grips with their true experiencing and to develop more meaningful and satisfying ways of living. Rogers believes that individuals have the capacity within them to discover what is making them anxious and unhappy and to bring about changes in their lives. This capacity may be latent, however, because of various negative parental and social forces; in such cases client-centered therapists may be able to help mobilize inherent tendencies toward personal understanding and growth. The therapist provides a warm, accepting atmosphere within which clients can express themselves openly. It is not the therapist's job to give advice or to "set the client straight." Rather, the task is to provide honest acceptance and understanding during the clients' struggles toward greater awareness of their inner experiencing and of the environmental influences that are affecting them.

Some of these ideas, and a realization of their uniqueness, crystallized for Rogers in 1940. There was an interplay between therapy and theory as he formulated hypotheses from his clinical practice and then attempted to substantiate these hypotheses in further clinical work. He felt that his clinical experiences provided considerable support for his views on human nature and the ways in which its development can be either stunted or fostered. Expanding on his findings as a therapist, he gathered additional support for his ideas as he moved into other areas of interest: encounter groups, intimate relationships, education, and conflict resolution. He continues to believe that his basic concepts are valid, and his ongoing experiences with people sustain this belief.

Rogers has not been satisfied with simply making subjective judgments about the validity of his theoretical assumptions. He and his colleagues have attempted to substantiate various hypotheses about the conditions favoring human growth and fulfillment by objectively studying the changes that occur in individuals during client-centered therapy. For example, recordings have been made, with clients' permission, of various sessions during the therapeutic process (Rogers and his students pioneered this approach in 1940). Through analysis of these recordings, it has been determined that there are certain typical and fairly orderly changes that take place under the conditions of interpersonal warmth and acceptance that exist in the client-centered therapeutic relationship: (1) verbal statements of "problems" and derogatory comments about oneself tend to diminish as therapy progresses, and (2) insightful and self-accepting statements (and, in some cases, statements indicating acceptance of others), as well as discussions of plans, goals, and decisions, tend to occur with increased frequency in later sessions. Of course, not all clients show this pattern, but Rogers has been encouraged by the number who do.

A method that has been applied in the study of changes in clients' concepts of themselves before, during, and after therapy is the *Q-sort*. At the beginning of therapy it is common for a large difference to exist between clients' perceptions of what they are like (the *self*) and their perceptions of what they feel they should be and want to be (the *ideal self*). This discrepancy between the self and the ideal self can be measured with the *Q*-sort, which provides an objective measure of the client's subjective experiencing. The client may be asked to sort 100 or so statements, each printed on a separate card. Statements such as "I am lazy," "I often feel guilty," "I am usually happy," and "I express my feelings openly" are put into various piles along a continuum ranging from one extreme ("very characteristic of me") to the opposite extreme ("not at all characteristic of me"). Typically the client has the opportunity to use from 9 to 11 different piles, with the middle pile the one for statements about which he or she feels neutral. The client may be told that a certain number of statements must be placed in each pile; this is to encourage discriminations among the statements as they relate to him or her and to facilitate statistical analyses.

When clients sort the statements first according to the way they see themselves at present (the *self-sort*) and then according to the way they feel they would like to be (the *ideal-sort*), the correspondence between their selves and their ideal selves can be computed quantitatively (using a statistical technique called *correlational analysis*). As mentioned previously, this procedure may be used before, during, and after therapy in order to measure changes in the discrepancy between the self and the ideal self. This discrepancy should decrease as client-centered therapy progresses; clients should become more the way they want to be and, to some extent, become less "idealistic" about what they *should* be. Even though these results haven't *always* been obtained, there has been some support for Rogers' hypotheses concerning positive changes in self-perceptions during therapy. What is most important here is that Rogers has attempted to provide objective, quantitative evidence for his assumptions.

It should be noted that Rogers has been quick to admit that his thinking is rooted in his particular cultural background—a democratic, Judeo-Christian tradition. His personal experiences, therapeutic work, and research have taken place mainly within this context. He does hope, however, that his ideas have universality. His goal is to develop certain basic concepts concerning human functioning that apply to all humans, although he knows that this is a difficult task. By attempting to make explicit assumptions about primary human characteristics, he feels that he is exposing these hypotheses for anyone to scrutinize and test.

What we have covered here are two major examples of research efforts to provide objective, scientific evidence for some of Rogers' assumptions. There are additional efforts that could be mentioned, some providing substantial support for Rogerian thinking and others yielding contradictory data. The main point is that his views remain viable, important, and well worth considering. Next to be discussed are a number of concepts that Rogers has developed to explain personality development and structure and that constitute his theory of personality. Some of these have been mentioned before.

It must be pointed out that Rogers has not made the construction of a personality theory his *primary* concern. His main focus has been on the process of personality change. Out of that central interest, however, certain ideas have emerged that do constitute a theory of personality. His theoretical concepts are primarily inferences drawn from his clinical experiences and other observations.

■ THE ACTUALIZING TENDENCY ■

According to Rogers, *the actualizing tendency is the single, basic human motive.* He believes that the human organism inherently tends to maintain itself and to strive for enhancement, and this is what he means by "actualization." The phrase "growth and fulfillment," used earlier, refers to major aspects of actualization and in general can be considered as synonymous with that term. Actualization, however, also includes maintenance of the organism.

In Rogers' view we are set at birth to grow productively toward fulfillment. We are basically active and forward moving, and, *if conditions are favorable,* we will attempt to develop our potentialities to their maximum. The specifics of human growth vary from person to person; in other words, not everyone will do exactly the same things when conditions are proper for actualization. To illustrate, one individual may choose to become intensely involved in family life and the nurturance of children, striving to heighten his or her experiences within that context, whereas another person may be heavily involved in increasing his or her professional competence and in developing meaningful non-marital relationships. Rogers suggests that there is no need to assume separate motives for these different behaviors; it is sufficient to posit one primary motive—*the actualizing tendency*—and then to go on and study the conditions under which actualization occurs, whatever this involves in terms of specific behaviors.

Although actualization differs from person to person with regard to specifics, there are still some generalizations that apply. Some common characteristics resulting from the actualization process are flexibility rather than rigidity, openness rather than defensiveness, and autonomy (increased freedom from external control) rather than heteronomy.

Rogers is *holistic* in his thinking, tending to look at the complete organism in order to understand and explain behavior. He conceptualizes a total functioning individual rather than trying to analyze each behavior as an isolated event. His concept of the actualizing tendency applies to the organism as a whole; this tendency is the *only* central source of energy, and it mobilizes the entire organism toward maintenance and enhancement. It involves (in addition to those things mentioned in the preceding praragraph) such areas as attempts to get air, water, food, and so on, the differentiation of the body's organs and functions, increased effectiveness in using tools and other cultural implements, and fulfillment through reproduction. The healthy human organism is moved toward greater and greater growth in its capabilities as a result of the actualizing tendency—*if* conditions exist that are conducive to this growth. Rogers stresses that developing individuals need to experience unconditional acceptance from other persons who are significant in their lives.

■ THE SELF AND SELF-ACTUALIZATION ■

The notion of *self* or *self-concept* is so important in Rogers' psychology that his theory is often referred to as a "self theory." The self is an outgrowth of certain aspects of individual experiencing. The newborn infant is an organism whose inner experiencing (also referred to as the *phenomenal field* or *subjective world*) is a relatively undifferentiated *totality* of sensations and perceptions that constitute his or her reality. As the actualizing tendency moves the infant toward maintenance and enhancement of experienced potentialities, interaction occurs with significant other persons (for example, the mother and father). As this happens, part of the infant's organismic experiencing differentiates into a "self" or "self-concept." Certain sensations and perceptions become discriminated as "I," "me," "myself" or as being related to "I," "me," "myself." These are *self-experiences.*

Rogers points out that there is a tendency for the self to be a fluid and changing totality, but at any given time it has certain properties that can be at least partially measured objectively by methods such as the *Q*-sort. As the self is portrayed here, it is a special part of the individual's total organismic experiencing. The person may not be fully aware at any given time of all experiencing that constitutes or relates to the self, but such awareness is a possibility.

Sometimes it is difficult to state something in simple terms without losing essential meanings. However, the following is an attempt to rephrase the two preceding paragraphs in easier-to-understand language and to make a few additional points: Infants at birth are not aware of themselves as unique entities, except perhaps in a very general way. As they develop and as their parents and other significant persons interact with them, there is a growing awareness in each child that there is something that is *him* or *her.* The child begins to make statements such as *"I* want . . . ," *"I* feel like . . . ," "Give that to *me,"* "This is *mine,"* and "Let *me* do it." These self-perceptions initially tend to be changeable, and the child sometimes feels '"happy," sometimes "insecure," sometimes "aggressive," and so on. Some persons continue to remain quite aware of many of their sensations, perceptions, feelings, thoughts, memories, and so on and incorporate a large number of these inner experiences into their self-concepts. Other persons develop more limited and static views of who and what they are. Rogers believes that humans have the potential to be aware of their total experiencing, but to do so requires openness and responsiveness to this experiencing;

this may or may not be encouraged by significant others (such as parents during childhood and marriage partners or close friends during adulthood). If significant others are accepting of the full variety of a person's inner experiencing, the self-concept of that individual is likely to be very "rich"—it will not have to be molded according to someone else's criteria (this topic will be discussed in more detail shortly).

As the self or self-concept develops, the actualizing tendency operates to actualize this emerging portion of the organism. Rogers refers to this as the tendency toward *self*-actualization. The *self-actualizing* tendency can be considered as a subsystem of the more basic *actualizing tendency*. (Remember, the actualizing tendency is the underlying organismic motive. The development of the self is an outgrowth of the general tendency toward maintenance and enhancement of the organism; as this self is forming, some of the actualizing tendency expresses itself in self-actualization.)

Before continuing, here is a summary of what has been said so far in this chapter: Rogers is *humanistic*, believing that humans are innately good and that they are growth oriented. He also holds a *phenomenological view*, which implies that it is important to understand an individual's perceptions of reality if his or her behavior is to be understood. He believes that *determinism* is an appropriate view for the scientist who is looking for cause-and-effect relationships but that it is essential in other circumstances to consider humans as having *freedom*. Rogers has pursued his study of humans both through objective research and through therapeutic and other subjective interpersonal relationships. A basic assumption in Rogerian psychology is that the *organism* (which can be considered as the locus of all experiencing—it is a more technical term than "human being") has an *actualizing tendency* as its single, basic, underlying motive. The actualizing tendency serves to maintain and enhance the organism's experiences and potentialities; that is, it encourages *actualization.* An outcome of the growth and elaboration of the organism is the development of a *self* or *self-concept.* Some of the actualizing tendency becomes invested in the expansion and fulfillment of the self or self-concept, and this subsystem of the actualizing tendency is referred to as the *self-actualizing tendency.*

■   THE ORGANISMIC VALUING PROCESS   ■

The organismic valuing process supplements the actualizing tendency. It is associated with actualization and helps to explain in more detail the positive direction of organismic growth.

In Rogers' opinion, the organismic valuing process in infants is very efficient and soundly based. The infant's values are very clear; preferences and dislikes are quite obvious. Experiences that maintain and enhance (actualize) the organism are preferred; experiences that do not actualize the organism are rejected. The infant values food positively when hungry and negatively when satiated. Positive values are generally associated with the warmth and security of "cuddling" and with new experiences, such as investigating his or her own body, learning to walk, and playing with new toys (as Rogers has pointed out, infants display an "endless curiosity"). Pain, sudden loud noises, and bitter tastes are negatively valued.

We start out in life *knowing* what we like and dislike and, generally speaking, what is good and not good for us. In the infant stage the valuing process is ongoing and flexible and operates smoothly. The criterion for whether something is positively or negatively valued rests on whether or not it maintains and/or enhances the organism and, once developed, the self. The valuing process at this early period of life functions spontaneously, without preconceived judgments or concerned and detailed thought.

Rogers believes strongly that we would all be better off if we were able to retain this kind of functioning—that is, if the organismic valuing process could continue to operate smoothly and flexibly. This evaluating process occurs *within the individual* and is intimately tied to inner experiences of desirability or undesirability *for the individual.* As mentioned above, each of us begins life subjectively knowing what is appropriate or inappropriate for our own development and fulfillment. What happens to this internal guide for living? Rogers points out that, by adulthood, many of us have lost contact with our organismic valuing process. We tend to become inflexible, uncertain, and uncomfortable in our values and often live unproductively with defensiveness and anxieties. Somewhere along the way to adulthood the inherent valuing process that should have led to ever more fruitful and fulfilling ways of living (that is, toward higher and higher levels of actualization) ceased to operate properly. Why? The answer to this question, which has already been hinted at, will now be discussed more fully.

■ UNCONDITIONAL POSITIVE REGARD ■

When the self develops, the individual wants love and acceptance; there is a need for *positive regard* from others. Rogers has suggested that this need for love and affection is innate (see Frick, 1971, p. 90). Because of this need, certain other persons in a child's life (and later in the adult's life) assume great importance. These significant others (for example, parents) can strongly influence the individual by giving and withholding love and acceptance, and their influence may overcome that of the organismic valuing process. In other words, to be accepted and to gain needed love and affection, the child may be forced to please parents and other significant persons and to ignore his or her own inner experiencing. The child may gradually become less and less "tuned in" to himself or herself and more and more a product of social influence. If other persons determine what is "right" or "wrong" and "good" or "bad," the role of the individual's organismic valuing process is usurped.

Early in life, then, we learn to view ourselves as others view us. We come to like or dislike our total configuration of self-experiences independently of the immediate presence of our parents or other significant persons. In other words, we incorporate within ourselves a set of values that initially was applied externally. The internalization of these values of significant others results in alienation from our own organismic valuing process.

The introjected values of others, which we come to live by to greater or lesser extents, generally tend to be rigid and unchanging, in contrast to the flexible and changing values of the organismic valuing process operating in early infancy. Rogers has suggested a number of introjected values that are often learned in the home, at school, in church, from the government, and so on; these values may be out of line with organismic experiencing, but they are often accepted in order to have the positive regard of significant other persons: (1) sexuality is bad; (2) unquestioning obedience to authority is good; (3) making money is very important; (4) scholarly learning is good; (5) unstructured, aimless learning is a waste of time; and (6) communism is totally bad. Other examples might be the common beliefs that it is improper for men to cry or hug each other and for women to be independent or assertive.

An important point is that the person's *self-regard* (one's view of one's own worth) is determined by these introjected values. As Rogers indicates, the individual "becomes in a sense his own significant social other" (see Rogers, 1959, p. 224). *Conditions of worth* develop in this way, so that the person has regard for himself or herself only when he or she thinks, feels, and acts in certain specified ways; other thoughts, feelings, and actions (which have not been accepted by significant others) are considered unworthy and tend to be excluded from one's self-concept in order to maintain self-regard. Some self-experiences may be excluded even though they are valid according to the organismic valuing process (that is, certain self-experiences may be rejected despite their actualizing value; the basic, natural maintenance and enhancement of the organism and self are therefore disregarded in favor of imposed standards).

The thoughts, feelings, and actions approved by significant others (and eventually approved by individuals themselves in order to maintain *positive regard* and *self-regard*) may be so different from the experiences approved by the person's own organismic valuing process that an almost complete dissociation develops between his or her self-concept and his or her most basic and fundamental inner experiencing. This situation is very unhealthy and causes the person to function in a restricted and inefficient way and to experience tension and anxiety.

Does the alienation of the person from the organismic valuing process have to occur? No, it does not, according to Rogers. However, in a world in which there are so many imposed values of good and bad, right and wrong, desirable and undesirable, it is highly unusual when an individual escapes the deadening influence of social norms and standards passed on by parents, teachers, employers, friends, marriage partners, and the other significant persons in one's life from whom acceptance is needed. Nevertheless, it is still hypothetically possible that individuals can remain in contact with the organismic valuing process and continue throughout life to maintain and enhance themselves according to their natural organismic potentialities. A necessary condition for this to happen is the experiencing of *unconditional positive regard*, which is one of the most significant concepts in Rogers' psychology.

Unconditional positive regard is *received* when a person perceives that all of his or her self-experiences (feelings, thoughts, sensations, and so on) are equally worthy of positive regard from significant others. Unconditional positive regard is *given* when all of the self-experiences of another person are valued equally; in other words, no conditions of worth are imposed on that individual. Rogers suggests that "acceptance" and "prizing" are generally synonymous with "unconditional positive regard." If another person is *accepted* or *prized*, that person is valued unconditionally; he or she is allowed awareness of the full range of inner experiencing and does not have to deny or reject any aspect of that experiencing in order to gain and maintain positive regard from others.

Unconditional positive regard should *not* be considered an absolute, all-or-nothing concept. It is probably impossible to experience complete unconditional positive regard *from* another person or *for* another person. It exists to greater or lesser extents in various interpersonal situations, and it can often be increased.

To clear up a possible area of confusion, it should be pointed out that, if a person is accepted or prized, it does not necessarily follow that all of his or her *behaviors* must be valued equally (see Rogers, 1959, p. 225). For example, hitting another person may be frowned on; but the person who hits, and the *desire* to hit, can be accepted. In this way, unconditional positive regard is maintained.

Following this line of reasoning, it would be possible for parents to express displeasure with certain of their child's actions, such as throwing food at the dinner table, beating up a younger sibling, banging on the wall with a hammer, being rude to a neighbor, or pulling the dog's tail, while at the same time making it known to the child that they accept the fact that he or she *wants* to do these things. That is, they would not let the child's behaviors interfere with their overall love or with their acceptance of the child's feelings.

Practical applications of unconditional positive regard are obviously quite difficult to accomplish at times. In the face of a child's (or anyone's) annoying and disruptive behaviors, it isn't always easy to be accepting of that individual's essential being. We often tend to get angry and threaten to withdraw love, affection, or acceptance. Yet anger needn't have the ill effects associated with withdrawing love; it is possible to "prize" others even though we are angered by them. (In Rogers' earlier writings the emphasis seemed to be on a rather even-tempered approach to others, specifically by therapists. Later he suggested that, *within the context of an accepting relationship,* a variety of emotions can be expressed mutually and productively even if anger or annoyance is involved (see Frick, 1971, p. 102).

A parent, teacher, or friend can convey to a child, student, or peer that love and acceptance are *not* at stake, despite the fact that annoyance, anger, or disapproval of a particular *behavior* is being expressed. It is important that respect for persons and their thoughts and feelings be maintained regardless of the specifics of the interaction at any given time. If this occurs, they should not have to cut themselves off from their inner experiencing, even though they may inhibit some disruptive behaviors.

The inhibition of behavior is most desirable when persons choose to do so as a reaction to their total experiencing, which might include the knowledge that a certain action will harm or displease someone else. As persons mature under circumstances of unconditional positive regard, they come more and more to be able to choose and decide on the basis of a complete flow of experiences; the organismic valuing process incorporates all sorts of factors, and the maintenance and enhancement of the organism and the self come to include considerations of the social consequences of behavior. In other words, persons can choose to act or not to act on the basis of their inner evaluations of the whole complex array of relevant internal and external factors, including the effects of their behaviors on others.

As will be made clear when client-centered therapy is discussed, unconditional positive regard is essential for a therapeutic relationship. The therapist must feel that the client is worthy of respect regardless of the client's feelings or behaviors. When clients are accepted for what they are, they can then begin to drop their defenses against, and denial of, self-experiences that have been disowned because of previous exposure to conditional, rather than unconditional, positive regard. Rogers' observations and studies of the positive changes that occur during the course of client-centered therapy have supported his belief in the effectiveness of unconditional positive regard.

■ CONGRUENCE AND INCONGRUENCE ■

Congruence is a state of consistency or harmony; *incongruence* is a state of discrepancy or disharmony. The concepts of congruence and incongruence in Rogers' theory grew out of his therapeutic experiences, as he observed clients struggling to revise their self-concepts in the direction of greater consistency with organismic experiencing. In other words, the clients were moving *from* a state of incongruence between their self-concepts and their organismic experiencing and *toward* a state of increasing congruence between these aspects of themselves. Rogers has suggested that the terms "integrated," "whole," and "genuine" can be considered synonymous with "congruent." A major goal of client-centered therapy is to allow the client to achieve a congruent state.

How does the self become incongruent with organismic experiencing? This question has been answered in part already. It is such a vital question, however, that reiteration and further clarification are warranted. Rogers has suggested that the alienation of the self from natural organismic experiencing (and the organismic valuing process) is the "basic estrangement" in humans.

This "basic estrangement" begins when conditional positive regard is experienced. The need for self-regard causes individuals to develop conditions of worth when love, affection, or acceptance from significant others is offered conditionally. They come to see themselves in essentially the same way that others see them: when they feel and behave "appropriately" (as initially defined by others), they maintain regard for themselves; when they feel or behave "inappropriately," their self-regard is lowered.

The person, because of conditions of worth, develops a selective self-concept; certain self-experiences are accepted, whereas others are rejected, denied, or distorted. Clear awareness of these latter experiences is lost. In other words, some organismic experiences are no longer allowed into consciousness as self-experiences (to put it another way, these experiences are no longer *symbolized*), or they are allowed into consciousness only in some misrepresented form (they are not accurately symbolized). As a result, there is a breach between one's self and one's organismic experiencing. Incongruence exists.

When the self-concept becomes incongruent, the implication is that there is also incongruence between the *self-actualizing* tendency and the more basic *actualizing* tendency. These tendencies then work at cross-purposes, because actualization of the incongruent self is not in keeping with actualization of the organism. (For example, self-actualization in the direction of introjected values of professional success and the attainment of wealth may be inconsistent, for some persons, with more basic actualization needs for warm interpersonal relationships and the freedom to explore alternative life-styles.) This situation can lead to stagnation of healthy development and to serious psychological discomfort—unless the person can somehow restore congruent functioning. The organismic valuing process falls into an inoperative state; this inner guiding voice no longer shows the way toward actualization. The person also loses freedom of choice. To choose effectively, the individual must be aware of inner experiencing and be able to test reality effectively. The incongruent personality is too threatened to bring into full awareness the vital aspects of organismic experiencing and environmental conditions; too much is "unacceptable" or "unpleasant" and therefore is defended against, denied, or distorted.

As Rogers points out, the person does not consciously get into a state of incongruence. Because the positive regard of others is needed, particularly during infancy, disharmony between the basic organism and the developing self generally begins early in life. This "basic estrangement" does not have to occur if the individual experiences unconditional positive regard.

■ THE FULLY FUNCTIONING PERSON ■

The concept of the "fully functioning person" is an ideal; according to Rogers, this hypothetical individual would represent the ultimate actualization of the human organism. Such a person would have experienced unconditional positive regard from significant others; no conditions of worth would exist, and therefore the individual would experience unconditional self-regard.

In actuality, no one has achieved this absolute state. People in real life are fully functioning in relative terms—some more, some less. Also, Rogers points out that it is best to conceive of full functioning as a *process* rather than as a static condition. A person who is functioning well is an adaptive organism, changing to meet new situations in the most satisfying ways and moving toward higher levels of actualization. So, even though the term "fully functioning" can be used in a hypothetical sense to refer to the ultimate in human development, it should be realized that Rogers is most concerned with the *process* of actualization. In a practical sense, a fully functioning person is one who is able to move constructively in the direction of ever-increasing growth and fulfillment.

Rogers considers the ideal fully functioning person to be in a state of congruence; no disharmony exists between the self and organismic experiencing. Such a person is accurately aware of inner experiencing and does not defend against or distort experiences. The fully functioning person effectively tests reality in order to maximize satisfactions, rather than "making do" with unsatisfying life conditions. Also, and very importantly, to be fully functioning is to be able to carry on relationships with others in harmonious ways.

Rogers has made it clear that persons who are sensitive to their total experiencing are very "trustworthy" beings; their behaviors benefit both themselves and society, and they make sound choices. Rogers' optimism about basic human nature is very strong. Fully functioning persons are "in tune" with this basic nature, and their reactions as they move through life are firmly grounded in their total organismic experiencing. To function fully is to function in a total organismic way, integrated and unified; it is *not* intellectual, self-conscious functioning.

Rogers believes that conscious and rational thought, on its own and out of touch with the totality of one's inner experiencing, is not an effective means of arriving at life's decisions. The fully functioning person chooses wisely because of intimate contact with the organismic valuing process. Rogers has pointed out at various times that "man is wiser than his intellect." This is not to degrade the human ability to reason but rather to indicate that humans function optimally when they operate as total, unified organisms—open and responsive to all their experiencing—rather than as *solely* cognitive, self-consciously rational beings. In short, we should be in touch with our basic feelings, sensations, and tendencies in such a way that they mix with reasoned considerations in a kind of fluid process, creating effectively integrated responses on the basis of total organismic functioning.

The most important factor in full functioning is the positive regard received from significant other persons, especially during the early years of life when we are most vulnerable. If love and acceptance are conditional and are experienced only when the "proper" feelings, thoughts, behaviors, and so on are expressed, then restricted, ineffective functioning is the likely outcome. If love and acceptance are unconditional and are experienced regardless of particular feelings, thoughts, behaviors, and so on, then full functioning is more likely.

What happens to persons who experience mainly conditional, rather than unconditional, positive regard? Are these individuals doomed to spend their entire lives in states of poor functioning, plagued by psychological discomforts and maladaptive behaviors? Not necessarily. Client-centered therapy, which has been referred to repeatedly, may possibly help such persons to regain contact with organismic experiencing and to reduce incongruence.

■ **CLIENT-CENTERED THERAPY** ■

Rogers has suggested that "psychotherapy is the releasing of an already existing capacity in a potentially competent individual" (see Rogers, 1959, p. 221). He emphasizes three attitudinal conditions that he believes are essential for an effective therapeutic relationship. (Although these conditions are stated in an absolute way, it should be understood that they are met to greater or lesser degrees in various client-centered therapy situations.) (1) *The therapist is congruent in the relationship—* that is, genuine, unified, and integrated, without defensive facades— and is able to meet the client on the basis of his or her (the therapist's) own organismic experiencing. There is harmony between what the therapist feels and what is communicated to the client. (2) *The therapist experiences unconditional positive regard for the client,* relating on a person-to-person basis while feeling that the client is a worthy individual, regardless of the client's condition, feelings, or behavior. The client is "prized" for what he or she is and may become. (3) *There is empathic understanding of the client.* The therapist's approach is phenomenological; the attempt is to sense the client's inner experiencing by entering and remaining within his or her subjective world. Rogers has indicated that the therapist should be sensitively involved with the client's experiencing and be able to convey effectively to the client that this experiencing is understood, but the therapist should not get bound up in anger, confusion, fear, or other emotions that the client may be feeling. Accurate sensing and sharing of the client's experiencing are essential, but the therapist should remain sufficiently disentangled from the emotional impact to allow clear perspectives to be maintained. In this way, the client can be helped to gain clearer perspectives.

The client-centered therapist attempts to create an atmosphere of warmth and acceptance in which clients can dismiss their fears of expressing themselves and come into increasingly closer contact with their organismic experiencing. Obviously, warmth and acceptance are not communicated to the client by simply stating that they exist; the therapist should actually *feel* that he or she unconditionally accepts and respects the client, and should *feel* empathic. Also, these feelings should be accurately experienced by the therapist; it is not a good situation if the therapist unconsciously feels uncomfortable and rejecting. In short, the therapist needs to be a fully functioning person. Attempts to artificially manipulate conditions in the therapeutic relationship will not be successful in producing changes in the client; the therapist has to be *real.*

To correct any misconceptions that a client-centered therapist has to be a superperson, perfect in every way, Rogers indicates that this is not the case. The characteristics mentioned in the preceding paragraphs are ideal characteristics. Even though therapists are not always completely congruent, accepting, and empathic, they can still be of help if they are able to be themselves in a relatively complete and full way. It is fortunate, as Rogers puts it, "that imperfect human beings can be of therapeutic assistance to other imperfect human beings" (see Rogers, 1959, p. 215). It is not unusual for a therapist to experience some uncertainties during a therapeutic relationship; the condition that is most likely to lead to failure is the therapist's defending against these uncertainties by denying or distorting their existence. If therapists are accurately aware of their own inner experiencing, including their feelings of discomfort, doubt, or fear, then there is less likelihood that harm will be done to the therapist-client relationship.

Should the therapist communicate such feelings directly and openly to the client? For example, should a therapist tell a client that something they are talking about has triggered a long-standing unresolved conflict or that he or she feels afraid because the client is expressing so much hostility? Interestingly, there has been a trend in client-centered therapy toward such open expressiveness on the part of the therapist. Perhaps by being more self-expressive, the client-centered therapist helps provide an even richer therapeutic relationship and may find it easier to maintain "realness" and sincerity in feelings toward the client. Of course, it is still of primary importance for the process of therapy to be focused on the *client's* unfolding discovery of his or her own inner experiencing; it is this unfolding that guides the therapeutic relationship, determining its pace and direction.

The basic problem that client-centered therapy is designed to resolve is the alienation of persons from their organismic experiencing and the organismic valuing process. Troubled clients have incorporated conditions of worth, resulting in conditional self-regard and incongruence between the self and organism. The self-actualizing tendency and the actualizing tendency are not operating in harmony. The client experiences anxiety because he or she is not functioning as a unified, integrated being.

The concept of *subception* is important here. In Rogers' theory, subception refers to the discrimination of an experience without full, clear awareness of that experience. Subception accounts for clients' feelings of threat from organismic experiences that are not fully conscious. In other words, when incongruence exists between the self and the organism, individuals are not clearly aware of their basic experiencing; still, they may be threatened by aspects of this experiencing that are inconsistent with self-concepts developed under the influence of conditional positive regard. Put more simply, we can be made to feel troubled by basic stirrings within us, even though we have pretty much cut ourselves off from these feelings and sensations in order to maintain positive regard from others and to maintain our own self-regard. Despite the fact that we have disowned them and do not accept them as being part of us (and therefore have lost clear and immediate contact with them), these feelings can still make us feel uncomfortable, threatened, or anxious. We *subceive*, rather than clearly *perceive*, these feelings and sensations, and they disturb our overly restricted self-concepts.

The major responsibility for change during client-centered therapy is on the client; it is the client who must rediscover his or her own inner experiencing and become sensitive once again to the directions indicated by the organismic valuing process. Rogers' assumption is that the client can do this if the therapist meets the three major attitudinal conditions mentioned earlier. By being congruent, accepting, and empathic, the therapist sets the stage for clients to examine, in a nonthreatening atmosphere, those inner experiences that are inconsistent with present self-concepts and that they are only dimly aware of (through subception) or aware of in some distorted way. Only the client can accomplish this—the therapist cannot do it for the client—and Rogers believes that humans have this capacity once the proper conditions are provided. (The therapist's role used to be called "nondirective," but this term has become misleading because of more active participation by client-centered therapists; also, as Rogers has suggested, the term does not sufficiently emphasize the therapist's focus on the factors that promote the client's growth.)

Three necessary attitudes on the part of the therapist have been indicated. But what about specifics? What does the therapist *do* during therapy? The responsibility is placed on clients to search out their own lost experiencing and to integrate this experiencing into their self-concepts so that they become more integrated and unified (congruent) beings, but how does the therapist behave during this process? Some of the communication during therapy is nonverbal; for example, the therapist may convey congruency, acceptance, and empathy through facial expressions. His or her verbal behavior is intended to clarify the feelings of the client, perhaps by restating something the client says. Also, the therapist's comments indicate that he or she is "with" the client—that is, that they are sharing involvement in the therapeutic relationship. What the therapist says is often phrased in a tentative way, so that the client can be the final judge of whether the therapist's comments are appropriate. The following dialogue is hypothetical and is meant merely to illustrate (in an oversimplified way) the kind of interchange that might take place between a client and a therapist:

> *Client:* I don't know why I'm so sensitive. . . . It just seems that everything . . . well, I don't know. For example, if my boss says the slightest thing about my work, I feel hurt. If my wife brings up some small fault, I react with a sort of pouting, and maybe I'll even get angry and . . . maybe even walk out of the house.
>
> *Therapist:* You have the feeling . . . you feel that you're too sensitive about what others say?
>
> *Client:* Yes, damn it! Why can't I be a man and either stand up and say that I *am* right or else admit that I'm wrong? No, not me. Why do I make such a big deal out of things? I just get this sinking

feeling inside and end up . . . well, just feeling all raw and exposed and stupid.

Therapist: It really hurts. . . . You'd like to react differently to criticism. . . . It really bothers you that you can't.

Client: You bet I would. This bad feeling that I get—it's not doing me any good. Or anybody else either. But how can I change? I've tried—boy, *have I tried!* It just seems that I get too emotional and can't see things straight—and end up doing the same things again and again . . . just keep on doing the same dumb things.

Therapist: M-hm . . . it just seems so hard to change. . . . Nothing changes—the bad feelings just keep happening. . . . Is that it?

Client: Yes, that's the way it is. I go on and on in the same pattern. I guess it's hard to admit to myself that I do have faults—that I'm not perfect—and I guess I just feel that people won't care about me if they see my faults. Maybe that's why I'm so sensitive. . . . Maybe it's because I don't want people to see any flaws—because maybe I'm afraid that they won't like me or respect me.

Therapist: I see . . . m-hm . . . you keep doing the same things because it's hard to admit that you might have some faults. And you feel afraid that perhaps others won't like you or respect you if they see your faults. . . . It's pretty tough to change, isn't it?

A written exchange between a therapist and a client misses much of the full dynamics of the real situation. The warmth and ongoing feelings, the length of pauses and hesitancies, the tone of the statements, and other critical features that characterize the therapeutic relationship are lost in the above account. Hopefully, however, something has been conveyed about the therapist's role as a clarifier and organizer of the client's expressions and as a person who cares about and accepts the client. By helping to set free the client's own capacities for actualization, the therapist aids the client's development in a deeply understanding but noninterfering way.

The desired outcome of client-centered therapy is a more fully functioning person—a person who is in immediate and accepting contact with deep, personal feelings and who is fluid, changing, and richly differentiated in reactions. This contrasts with the functioning that often characterizes clients at the beginning of therapy, when they tend to be out of contact with real feelings and are more rigid and static. This change in functioning can be observed during the therapeutic process as the client moves away from more past-oriented, intellectually toned statements and toward statements that are more expressive of basic, immediate experiencing in the here-and-now.

It should be pointed out that successful therapy, regardless of the method used, often is hard to define. Since it is not possible at present

to measure precisely all the important dimensions of human functioning, it is difficult to make definite statements about the general effectiveness of client-centered therapy (or any other kind of therapy). Rogers and many others, however, are convinced that the successes of
client-centered techniques are sufficient to warrant enthusiastic, continued use. Meanwhile, research on the effectiveness of various ther-
apies continues, with attempts to develop better ways of measuring
outcomes.

Although client-centered therapy is Rogers' best-known contribution
to psychology, his concerns have gone far beyond individual-therapy
situations. He has been very interested in intensive group experiences
as a means of allowing individuals to experience more deeply and mean-
ingfully and to enrich their interpersonal relationships. He also has
been concerned with the dynamics of intimate relationships, such as
marriages. Other major interests are education and the problems of
maintaining world peace.

It is clear that Rogers has continued to expand his thinking into
significant areas of human experiencing, retaining certain fundamental ideas but pushing forward toward fresh applications of those ideas.
Let's look next at two of the areas just mentioned: encounter groups
and intimate relationships. The topics of education and world peace
will be discussed in the Commentary section.

■   ENCOUNTER GROUPS   ■

An encounter group is a small group that, through intense interaction,
allows individuals to find out more about themselves and the way they
relate to others. Rogers is greatly interested in the potential of these
groups for helping individuals to become more fully functioning.
Although encounter groups may have therapeutic value, they usually
are differentiated from "group therapy": the latter is designed to help
persons who have more serious problems and who are in more immediate need of assistance. Encounter groups typically are designed for
improving the capacities of those who already are functioning fairly
normally. ("Normal functioning" may not represent a very high level of
human potential. In other words, so-called normal persons may not be
living life nearly as fully as they could be, and encounter groups provide
one possible means of increasing personal growth.)

The size of an encounter group typically varies from about 8 to 15
members (although Rogers has conducted encounter-type workshops
with as many as 800 persons; see his book A Way of Being, pp. 316–335).
Sometimes a group may meet for one long session; in other cases, the
group may meet for a number of shorter sessions. Generally, there are
from 20 to 60 hours of intensive contact. No specific agenda is made
up beforehand; the setting is unstructured, so that the members can

freely investigate their feelings and their interactions with others through the evolving group process. Although there may be hostile exchanges and periods of much discomfort during the experience, the overall context is supposed to be one of mutual acceptance and helpfulness.

There is a great deal of controversy concerning the encounter-group phenomenon. Some persons vehemently tout the beneficial outcomes of these group experiences, others just as strongly oppose them, and still others hold more moderate opinions. Rogers is not a fanatic in his belief in the possibilities offered by intensive group experiences, but he does strongly support them, with certain reservations (to be mentioned later). He believes that they can lead to increased awareness of inner experiencing and can help individuals to develop more satisfying interpersonal relations. He also feels that they can be useful for a variety of purposes (such as reducing interpersonal and intergroup conflict) in a number of different settings, including government, industry, schools, churches, and the family.

Many different methods are used by group "facilitators" (this is one of the terms used to refer to encounter-group leaders, who do not "lead" the group in the traditional sense). A facilitator generally is concerned with providing an atmosphere in which persons can openly express themselves and can focus on their own experiencing and on their exchanges with others in ways that give fresh perspectives. Our concern in the following discussion is with Rogers' way of facilitating encounter groups.

He begins the encounter in a very unstructured way, making some comment such as "Here we are. We can make of this group experience exactly what we wish." He sets no specific goals and allows the group to determine its own direction. Rogers points out that this approach is very similar to the one he has used in client-centered therapy, although he tends to be more expressive in encounter groups than he was in one-to-one therapy situations. (Rogers is no longer actively involved in individual therapy but has indicated that, if he were, he would be more expressive and spontaneous than he was previously. He maintains that this is a result of the personal growth he has experienced in groups. He likes to be as much a participant as a facilitator when he is involved in a group.)

The following are some of the attributes that, according to Rogers, characterize him as a group facilitator: (1) *He listens carefully and sensitively,* considering each person as having something worthwhile to say. He is most interested in the present meanings and feelings that accompany members' expressions. Rogers feels that clear and respectful listening on his part helps to create a psychologically safe climate; thus, individuals should feel more comfortable about taking some risks in disclosing important aspects of themselves. (2) *He accepts both the group and individuals.* He has patience in allowing the group to "find itself" and to discover the directions it wants to follow. Also, he personally is willing to have members enter into the group's process to greater or lesser extents; if someone wants to stay on the sidelines, Rogers is not disapproving (sometimes other group members may disapprove, however, and put pressure on a stand-offish person). He also tends to accept what individuals say at face value and thus avoids "reading in" meanings or attributing unconscious motives. (3) *He attempts to be empathically understanding.* He believes that it is extremely important to understand from the other person's point of view what is being expressed. (4) *He operates in terms of his own feelings.* Rogers points out that he has become increasingly free in using the feelings that he has toward himself, other group members, or the group as a whole. He usually feels genuine concern for others and is especially empathic if someone is hurt psychologically. Expressions of feelings may include anger, annoyance, and frustration, as well as affection and love, especially if these feelings are persistently experienced by him.

Rogers emphasizes the expression of presently existing feelings, so that reactions are to the here-and-now. Divulging honest feelings may be painful to oneself or to others, but Rogers believes that this pain often can be growth producing. However, if he sees that someone is experiencing a great deal of distress, he gives the person the opportunity to say that he or she has had enough for a while. Rogers also thinks that facilitators should not be reluctant to express their own problems to the group and should let it be known if they are upset. (The exception to this advice is if the facilitator develops a severe personal problem, in which case it is probably best not to take the group's time to deal with it; rather he or she should seek help from colleagues or from other persons outside the group.)

What happens if someone in the group becomes seriously disturbed—perhaps because defenses have been broken down too quickly, causing sudden awareness by the individual of something that is extremely devastating to his or her previously protected self-concept? Rogers believes that encounter groups have great therapeutic potential (although, as mentioned previously, therapy is not the group's primary function). He has great trust in the group's ability to cope wisely with disturbances—even with pathological behavior—if the group is functioning well in general.

Rogers grants that other facilitators may find that different approaches work for them. He does caution, however, against certain procedures that he feels are unwise for a facilitator to use: (1) pushing or manipulating the group toward some specific, but unstated, goal; (2) emphasizing dramatic performances by group members; (3) emphasizing attacks by group members on one another and continually insisting on the expression of hostility; (4) frequently interpreting members' motives; (5) pressuring members to engage in certain exercises or activities without giving them a real chance to decide for themselves whether they want to participate; (6) remaining aloof from emotional participation in the group process and acting like an expert who has the ability to perform superior analyses of the group or of individuals. In addition, Rogers suggests that the person who has serious personal problems should steer away from the role of facilitator.

What is the typical process of an encounter group? Of course, not all groups behave in exactly the same way, but there are certain patterns that are fairly common. During the *early stages*, there tends to be confusion and perhaps anxiety about what the group is supposed to do. The unstructured atmosphere may be threatening to those who are used to having definite goals or procedures. There is often a great reluctance to go beyond superficialities. The notion of simply being together with a small number of other people to talk about whatever comes to mind, or to try to open up to others about personal concerns, is not easy to handle for many persons. After a time, however, certain group members generally begin to make hesitant moves toward expressing their feelings. They may talk about their reactions to the situation, their reasons for being there, their desire to get the group going in some direction, and so on. Some members may express annoyance or frustration with the group's lack of structure or, on the other hand, may "put down" someone who is trying to become the group's leader. As more and more feelings are expressed, persons who are holding back may be encouraged by others to speak out and to get involved in the interactions; continued resistance to active participation by a group member may bring accusations from others of defensiveness or aloofness.

During the *middle stages*, there is a tendency toward increasing honesty and mutual trust. Some of the earlier suspiciousness, impatience, and other confused and negative feelings start to be replaced by feelings of group unity and supportiveness for the exploration of both personal and interpersonal experiencing. Members begin to make perceptive comments about their own experiencing and become more empathic about the experiencing of others; it is at this point that the real possibilities for growth and heightened functioning begin to emerge. By being in a supportive atmosphere, in which spontaneity and the dropping of defenses are encouraged, the group members have the opportunity to see themselves in clearer and more honest ways, although there may be a great deal of discomfort when revealing some long-hidden personal problem or conflict. Also, each person can get feedback from others, perhaps gaining unique insights into the ways in which his or her behavior is perceived and the effects that it has on other persons. Some feedback may not be favorable, and this may lead to anxiety, anger or great hurt. However, the group's members have the potential to deal effectively with these reactions by reaching out to each other in honest, accepting ways and by developing empathic understanding.

By the time the *later stages* of the group process are reached, there often are feelings of great closeness and supportiveness among the members as an outgrowth of the sharing of deep experiencing. They have encountered one another with degrees of openness, responsiveness, and intimacy that are unique in this society. For perhaps the first time in their adult lives, they have allowed themselves and others to express ongoing inner experiences in a straightforward, honest way. They have allowed themselves to "be themselves," without the pretense and superficial social niceties that normally characterize interpersonal situations, and they have found that they are accepted by others even when their most basic feelings are revealed. If someone made them uncomfortable, they were allowed to say so; if they felt shy or inhibited, they were given the chance to "come out of their shells"; if some problem or conflict was bothering them, they could "get it off their chests." In short, facades have been dropped and real selves have surfaced without negative consequences; significant lessons have been learned with regard to individual experiencing and interpersonal behavior. (The picture being painted here is, of course, an ideal one. Some groups are more successful than others in achieving these outcomes.)

An encounter group should increase the actualization of its members. They should be more fully functioning after this intensive group experience, and there should be less incongruence between their self-concepts and their organismic experiencing. This does not necessarily mean that achievement of all-around happiness (whatever that is) is a goal. The group process is intended to open up individuals to new dimensions of experiencing, thereby setting the stage for continued growth. Some of this growth may be painful, but life changes often *are* painful. Learning to be oneself, dealing honestly with others, admitting long-inhibited fears, and so on can be upsetting and depressing and can cause unhappiness. However, it can also be deeply satisfying and fulfilling to face oneself and the world openly and to develop independence and the courage to choose one's own life patterns.

Rogers believes that the research evidence presently available indicates that most encounter-group experiences are positive. (Not all psychologists would agree with this conclusion.) He is also cautious, however, and among the shortcomings he has pointed out are the following, some of which may be remedied in the future by improved procedures: (1) the effects tend to be short-lived; (2) sometimes individuals may be left with unresolved problems; (3) the possibility exists that a group member may experience a psychotic episode; (4) a husband or wife who is involved in a group experience may change in ways that are disturbing to the spouse or may leave the group experience with unresolved sexual feelings toward another group member; (5) individuals who join a number of encounter groups may try to "run things" in new situations, thereby interfering with the natural group process (Rogers feels that this is especially likely to happen if such persons have been in phony-type groups); and (6) higher-status persons may have more difficulty than lower-status persons in letting down their defenses—they may feel that they have more to risk—and, when they finally do, the situation may be quite explosive. Obviously Rogers is not blind to the risks that are involved in intensive group experiences. Yet he feels that well-facilitated encounter groups are sufficiently beneficial to warrant their continued use. More research needs to be done, however, before anyone can claim with assurance that encounter groups are an unqualified success, and more follow-up studies are needed to indicate with greater precision the immediate and long-range effects of group participation.

■ INTIMATE RELATIONSHIPS ■

In his 1972 book, *Becoming Partners: Marriage and Its Alternatives*, Rogers attempts to delineate the critical aspects of successful intimate relationships. His method is phenomenological in that he focuses on the experiencing of those involved in these relationships, carefully examining interview and written material supplied to him by various couples. His emphasis is on marriages, but the implications of what he says are also relevant to other close, long-lasting relationships. Some of the couples he studied were relatively monogamous, whereas others were more open in sexual expression, with one or both partners having extramarital relations. Rogers cautions strongly against holding traditional notions of what is most desirable in a marriage; he feels that a wide variety of possibilities exists and that couples should be free to search for the most satisfying and fulfilling life-styles for *them.*

From interviews and the written material he received, Rogers extracted certain elements that he feels are present in meaningful, relatively permanent, growth-oriented relationships: (1) individual commitment to the changing process of the relationship, which leads to working together in the here-and-now because mutual enrichment is experienced and growth is desired; (2) communication of persistent inner feelings, even at the risk of disturbing the relationship, and empathic understanding of the partner's response; (3) dissolution of roles, so that behaviors in the relationship can evolve rather than being determined by prior expectations such as "A wife should . . ." or "A husband should . . ."; and (4) discovery and sharing of separate, strong, and independent selves, with each partner becoming more and more accurately aware and accepting of his or her experiencing.

It should be noted that Rogers is again emphasizing certain themes that are familiar throughout his writings: living should be an ongoing process rather than something static; reactions should be to here-and-now situations; inner experiencing should be clearly perceived and expressed; empathy is important; individuals should develop their own life-styles without having to live by outwardly imposed standards and values; and the discovery and development of one's unique self are vital for good functioning.

■   **COMMENTARY**   ■

Rogers' therapeutic approach was called *nondirective* in its earlier stages. Later it became widely known (as it still is) as *client-centered.* Many psychologists and others remain attached to the client-centered label, though Rogers and his colleagues, since the middle 1970s, have used the name *person-centered.* The point of the name change is to reflect more strongly that the *person,* in his or her full complexity, is at the center of focus. Also, Rogers and his colleagues want to emphasize that their assumptions are meant to apply broadly to almost all aspects of human behavior and are not limited to therapeutic settings. Two examples of broad applications of the person-centered approach are Rogers' suggestions regarding education and conflict resolution. Both of these areas have been of concern to him for many years, and he continues to write and speak about them.

His views on education follow his basic assumption that persons are able to direct their own lives if the proper conditions exist. He advocates that teachers be "facilitators" of learning, providing an atmosphere of freedom and support for individual pursuits. The facilitating teacher has the same attitudes as the effective therapist: he or she is genuine, accepting, and empathic. When students can choose their own paths to discovery, and are encouraged to do so, Rogers believes that real learning is likely to occur. Also, he stresses that learning should involve feelings as well as ideas; students who respond emotionally as well as cognitively learn most effectively. (Rogers' views on education obviously are quite different from Skinner's, although both want to promote better learning.)

During recent years, Rogers has devoted considerable effort to the problems of reducing conflicts and maintaining peace in a world threatened by nuclear war (he warns against trivializing nuclear horrors, as illustrated by video games that treat war and destruction playfully).[1] He believes that the conditions necessary for establishing peaceful relations between opponents are similar to those in encounter groups. That is, if enemies can meet face to face for a prolonged period to discuss openly their differences in an informal way, conflict is likely to subside.

[1] For example, see his article "Nuclear War: A Personal Response," *APA Monitor,* August 1982, pp. 6–7. Also in the *APA Monitor,* November 1984, p. 15, is an informative report on his work in this area.

The goals in such a situation, Rogers suggests, are to get each side to listen to and accept the hostile attitudes of the other, to break down the "I'm right and you're wrong" pattern, and to get each side to focus on the personal and human characteristics of the other. He gives the real-world example of the Camp David agreements between former Egyptian President Sadat and former Israeli Prime Minister Begin as evidence of what can happen if conditions are favorable. In Rogers' view, the relative informality of that situation, former President Carter's facilitative efforts, and the intensive contact between the men were critical factors that brought about effective communication and greater mutual understanding.

As beneficial as the person-centered approach might be if applied intentionally in a wide variety of situations, from interpersonal to international, Rogers sees difficulties in achieving general acceptance of his ideas. A theme in his book *Carl Rogers on Personal Power* is that the person-centered approach raises "political" issues; that is, it has to do with power, control, and decision making at many levels and is, therefore, revolutionary. Since it is revolutionary, Rogers believes, it threatens established authorities (professionals, administrators, and so on), who consciously and unconsciously want to destroy it.

The person-centered approach, wherever it exists, puts control for people's lives into their own hands. According to this view, persons can and should be trusted to make responsible decisions, and it is assumed that this can occur at every level of society. Rogers suggests that individuals, groups, and organizations function best (and society as a whole benefits) when the strength and wisdom that reside within persons are tapped and allowed to flow outward into constructive actions. Whereas social institutions can now be seen as exerting a great deal of direct, and often coercive, control over persons, Rogerian psychology maintains that this is neither healthy nor productive in the long run. At whatever social level persons are functioning, and in whatever role they find themselves, they should be in touch with their inner experiencing and should be relating to others in accepting, empathic, and genuine ways.

As noted in the previous chapters, Freud and Skinner have suggested broad social applications of their approaches. Rogers also has moved his ideas out of the relatively specific situations in which they were developed and has attempted to show that they have a vast amount of generality. At this point in time, the concepts of each of these three theorists are viable and their implications for complex social problems are worthwhile considering. (It can be argued, however, that they are not *equally* viable and worthwhile; sharp disagreements exist about this.)

At the level at which Rogers' ideas were developed originally, in therapy and counseling situations, his impact certainly has been significant and far-reaching. A wide range of individuals—psychotherapists, counselors, social workers, ministers, and others—have been influenced by Rogers' assumption that, if one can be a careful and accurate listener, while showing acceptance and honesty, one can be of help to troubled persons.

Perhaps part of Rogers' influence is due to the fact that his therapeutic approach appears to ensure, at the very least, that no further damage will be done. Rather than taking the chance that direct advice and guidance will be inappropriate, thereby creating additional problems, the therapist or counselor may prefer to take the Rogerian stance, which puts responsibility for change on the client. Critics, of course, could point out that this attitude *can* lead to further damage if the client does not take corrective action quickly enough or if he or she makes a bad decision. According to Rogers, however, constructive change can come about only when clients choose their courses of action by being in touch with their own basic experiencing. One person cannot decide or choose wisely for another person.

Rogers has a strong following among those who are not trained professionally at the doctorate level in psychology. This popularity has been stimulated by his position that professionals are not always the best qualified to help others. He believes that the essential conditions of unconditional acceptance, empathy, and genuineness often can be provided by those who have little or no formal training. Conversely, not all highly trained mental-health professionals are capable of providing these conditions, since their training has often emphasized techniques instead of ways of relating. This position has endeared him to many who resent the assumption that professional credentials are necessary in order to provide therapy and related services.

Rogers' optimistic focus on the positive aspects of human nature also has contributed much to his popularity, at least among those who share his hopeful outlook. His view has been compared to a fresh breeze, purifying and refreshing. Asked about his optimism, he once replied that it could be glandular (see Evans, 1975, p. 71). He went on to point out that he always has been interested in growth, whether it be in plants or in animals. One of his favorite activities is gardening, and he sees similarities between plants that grow well when conditions are favorable and persons who flourish when their circumstances support growth. (Could water, fertilizer, and adequate sunshine for plants be likened to unconditional positive regard, empathy, and congruence for people?)

The apparent simplicity of Rogers' approach is another aspect of its wide appeal. He sees no need to probe deeply into unconscious layers of the personality, to provide insightful interpretations, to analyze dreams, to use involved behavioral manipulations, or to use psychological tests to diagnose and categorize problems. The key to helping

another person is to establish an honest relationship, involving unpos-
sessive caring and empathic understanding. According to Rogers, what
is happening here and now, in the dynamic interaction between individuals who are attempting to respond to each other on the basis of
their real inner experiencing, is critical for producing healthful changes.
Through such relationships, persons are able to discover their own
hidden feelings and to become more fully functioning. For those who
are in positions of helping others, this approach seems clear and understandable, free from complicated concepts and procedures. Of course,
in actual practice, things often are not so simple; maintaining positive
regard, empathy, and genuineness can be very difficult. However, the
point remains that the essential ideas of the person-centered approach
are appealingly simple and straightforward. (A Freudian might want
to substitute the word "appallingly" for "appealingly" in the preceding
sentence.)

The growth-producing conditions of unconditional positive regard,
empathy, and congruence or genuineness have been mentioned time
and again. To a large extent, these conditions are interrelated. For
example, genuineness is necessary if the therapist is to be strongly
accepting and empathic. Though they are interdependent, Rogers has
suggested that one condition may be more important than another,
depending on the situation (see Holdstock and Rogers, 1983, p. 208).
Genuineness may be most important in everyday interactions; unconditional positive regard may be most important in parent-infant situations or in therapeutic settings involving psychotic clients; in typical
helping relationships, empathy appears to be the most crucial element.
For maximum benefits, however, all three conditions should exist to a
substantial degree. Some studies have indicated that the more a client
perceives these aspects of the therapeutic relationship, the greater the
client's gains.

Rogers' contributions have been significant, especially in the areas
of psychotherapy and counseling. His approach has proved to be a
useful one, and it has stimulated research efforts to try to validate its
basic assumptions about the conditions and processes of healthful
change. Still, the potential of the person-centered approach as a major
social force is not known. Limited attempts have been made to evaluate
its applications in marriages, educational systems, industries, community organizations, and so on, but these situations are very complex; it's difficult to pinpoint the critical determinants of constructive
change, even when such change does occur.

Though Rogers and his colleagues have been favorably impressed
with the results of larger-scale applications of the person-centered
approach, there are numerous skeptics who are less easily convinced.
Also, some of the same features of Rogerian psychology that many have
found attractive—its placement of responsibility for change on persons

themselves, its deemphasis on the need for professional credentials, its strongly optimistic view of human nature, and its relatively simple concepts and procedures with regard to therapy—have turned off others, both inside and outside the field of psychology. Only the future can decide whether the advocates or the detractors are closer to being correct.

■   REFERENCES FOR CHAPTER 4   ■

Primary Sources (Rogers' Own Writings)

1. *Counseling and Psychotherapy.* Boston: Houghton Mifflin, 1942.
2. Some observations on the organization of personality. *American Psychologist,* Vol. 2, September 1947, pp. 358–368.
3. *Client-Centered Therapy.* Boston: Houghton Mifflin, 1951. (Also in paperbound edition.)
4. "Client-centered" psychotherapy. *Scientific American,* November 1952, pp. 66–74.
5. The necessary and sufficient conditions of therapeutic personality change. *Journal of Consulting Psychology,* Vol. 21, No. 2, 1957, pp. 95–103.
6. A theory of therapy, personality, and interpersonal relationships, as developed in the client-centered framework. In S. Koch (Ed.), *Psychology: A Study of a Science.* Vol. 3. New York: McGraw-Hill, 1959. Pp. 184–256.
7. *On Becoming a Person.* Boston: Houghton Mifflin, 1961. (Also in paperbound edition.)
8. Actualizing tendency in relation to "motives" and to consciousness. In M. R. Jones (Ed.), *Nebraska Symposium on Motivation.* Lincoln: University of Nebraska Press, 1963. Pp. 1–24.
9. Toward a science of the person. In T. W. Wann (Ed.), *Behaviorism and Phenomenology.* Chicago: University of Chicago Press, 1964. Pp. 109–140. (Also in paperbound edition.)
10. Dealing with psychological tensions. *Journal of Applied Behavioral Science,* Vol. 1, No. 1, January-February-March 1965, pp. 6–24.
11. Autobiography. In E. G. Boring & G. Lindzey (Eds.), *A History of Psychology in Autobiography.* Vol. 5. New York: Appleton-Century-Crofts, 1967. Pp. 343–384.
12. *Person to Person: The Problem of Being Human.* Coauthored by Barry Stevens, with contributions from E. T. Gendlin, J. M. Shlien, & W. Van Dusen.) Lafayette, Calif.: Real People Press, 1967. (Also in paperbound edition by Pocket Books.)
13. The group comes of age. *Psychology Today,* December 1969, pp. 27–31, 58–61.
14. *Becoming Partners: Marriage and Its Alternatives.* New York: Delacorte, 1972. (Also in paperbound edition.)
15. The person of tomorrow. In G. B. Carr (Ed.), *Marriage and Family in a Decade of Change.* Reading, Mass.: Addison-Wesley, 1972. Pp. 3–8. (Paperbound.)

16. A humanistic conception of man. In G. B. Carr (Ed.), *Marriage and Family in a Decade of Change.* Reading, Mass.: Addison-Wesley, 1972. Pp. 8–24. (Paperbound.) Originally published in R. E. Farson (Ed.), *Science and Human Affairs.* Palo Alto, Calif.: Science and Behavior Books, 1965.

17. *Carl Rogers on Personal Power.* New York: Delacorte, 1977. (Also in paperbound edition.)

18. *A Way of Being.* Boston: Houghton Mifflin, 1980. (Paperbound.)

19. *Freedom to Learn for the 80's.* Columbus, Ohio: Merrill, 1983. (Paperbound.)

Secondary Sources

1. Evans, Richard I. *Carl Rogers: The Man and His Ideas.* New York: Dutton, 1975. (Paperbound.)

2. Frick, Willard B. *Humanistic Psychology: Interviews with Maslow, Murphy, and Rogers.* Columbus, Ohio: Merrill, 1971. Chapter 3, pp. 86–115. (Paperbound.)

3. Hall, Calvin S., & Lindzey, Gardner. *Theories of Personality.* (3rd ed.) New York: Wiley, 1978. Chapter 8, pp. 279–309.

4. Hall, Mary H. A conversation with Carl Rogers. *Psychology Today,* December 1967, pp. 19–21, 62–66.

*5. Holdstock, T. L., & Rogers, Carl R. Person-centered theory. In Raymond J. Corsini and Anthony J. Marsella, *Personality Theories, Research, & Assessment.* Itasca, Ill.: Peacock, 1983. Chapter 5, pp. 189–227.

6. Kirschenbaum, Howard. *On Becoming Carl Rogers.* New York: Delacorte, 1979.

*7. Meador, Betty D., & Rogers, Carl R. Person-centered therapy. In Raymond J. Corsini (Ed.), *Current Psychotherapies.* (3rd ed.) Itasca, Ill.: Peacock, 1984. Chapter 5, pp. 142–195.

8. Pervin, Lawrence A. *Personality: Theory and Research.* (4th ed.) New York: Wiley, 1984. Chapters 5 and 6, pp. 149–211.

9. Wood, John. Carl Rogers, gardener. *Human Behavior,* Vol. 1, No. 6, November/December 1972, pp. 16–22.

*Although Rogers appears as coauthor, he has indicated that the first author did the writing. Rogers served as a consultant and gave his approval to the final product.

Comparisons, Contrasts, Criticisms, and Concluding Comments

COMPARISONS AND CONTRASTS

There are various ways to compare and contrast the views of Freud, Skinner, and Rogers. The following discussions center on certain important issues in relating these three psychologies to one another. Some points will be familiar from preceding chapters.

Views of Basic Human Nature

FREUD made very strong assumptions about basic human nature. He posited powerful inherent factors that create tensions demanding relief: the sexual drive and the aggressive drive (which emerge, respectively, from the life and death instincts) urge humans toward selfish satisfactions. Freud tended to be quite pessimistic about human nature and was skeptical about our future. With the unconscious forces of sex and aggression pushing for gratification, humans can survive only if society inhibits or redirects these energies. To Freud, we are basically "savage beasts," and only the processes of civilization can bring wanton sexuality and destructiveness under control (for elaboration on this and the following points, see Freud's *Civilization and Its Discontents*).

The problem is not solved by socialization, however, since this process contradicts our instinctive self-seeking tendencies, which continue to generate various degrees of tension. In tracing human history, Freud suggests that one of the reasons why people first submitted themselves

133

to social control was to gain protection from one another, but this gain leads to the loss of happiness that could be obtained from unbridled self-indulgence. Thus, the unconscious is continually at war with civilization's controlling rules and values. Because Freud doubted that this conflict could ever be completely resolved, he suggested that civilization must use the processes of identification (incorporation of others' values, especially the parents') and sublimation (channeling of instinctual energies into socially desirable activities) to combat basic human nature. Psychoanalytic therapy is intended to strengthen the ego (the conscious, rational aspect of the human personality) so that it can both acknowledge and control instinctive, impulsive tendencies and attempt to find appropriate outlets for them—that is, outlets that are neither personally nor socially destructive.

SKINNER makes few assumptions about human nature, but he does grant that each person inherits a genetic structure that yields both general characteristics of the human species and unique characteristics of the individual. Rather than dwelling on the possible nature of these inborn propensities, Skinner quickly moves out to the environment and emphasizes the effects of environmental variables on human behavior, including the internal behaviors of feeling and thinking. His approach is aimed at exhausting the explanatory power of external variables.

One of the few specific assumptions about human nature that Skinner has offered is the idea that, because of our evolutionary history, we are reinforced by effectively manipulating our environment (since this characteristic has survival value, he suggests that it has become a genetic feature of the human species). In Skinnerian psychology, then, the genetic endowment of humans does determine that certain conditions will be reinforcing. Also, it determines the range of behaviors that we are capable of emitting.

In most important respects, Skinner considers the human organism to be controlled by the environment; therefore, the basic qualities of human nature are neither good nor bad. With regard to the behaviors that are typically considered to be important in assessing our fellow humans (aggression, sympathy, altruism, jealousy, love, and so on), Skinner's position emphasizes that they are mainly effects of external conditions. Complex behaviors do *not* arise from some source within humans, and they are not accounted for by referring to "human nature." As individuals, we are primarily what our environmental histories, and our presently existing circumstances, make us.

ROGERS makes definite assumptions, emphasizing that humans are naturally growth oriented and will progress toward fulfillment if conditions are favorable. He is optimistic, rather than pessimistic or neutral, about our essential characteristics and feels that the freedom to develop these characteristics results in positive and beneficial behaviors. At the theoretical level, Rogers' "growth-motivated person" is quite different from Freud's "tension-reducing person" or Skinner's "environmentally controlled person."

In Rogers' eyes, basic human nature can and should be trusted. It is only when individuals become alienated from their basic nature that they become personally or socially harmful. His position clearly suggests that persons should have the freedom to choose and should make decisions on the basis of their own inner experiencing. On the other hand, Freud stressed the need for the control and sublimation of basic impulses if civilization is to survive, while Skinner emphasizes the need for well-structured environments that shape and maintain desirable behaviors (to Skinner, basic human nature, or genetic endowment, is a biological system on which the environment acts).

At the risk of some oversimplification, it can be suggested that, with regard to their views of basic human nature, Rogers is an optimist, Freud was essentially pessimistic, and Skinner is neutral.

Views of Personality Development

FREUD emphasized psychosexual stages of development (oral, anal, phallic, latent, and genital) through which we move more or less successfully. We are set at birth to pass through these stages, during which there is a vital interaction between our strong inherent nature (as reflected, for example, in sexual and aggressive impulses) and factors involved in nurture (for example, toilet-training procedures, parents' behaviors toward sexuality, and strength of parental love). Early childhood, up to age 5 or 6, is of critical and lasting importance in the determination of the personality's structure and dynamics; the first three stages—oral, anal, phallic—are the most significant and strongly affect later development.

SKINNER sees a continual action of the environment on the individual. What is happening now (for example, present reinforcement contingencies) may be as important in determining behavior as what happened in the past. The person's behavior repertoire, which in Skinnerian psychology is what "personality" consists of, results from the consequences of behaviors emitted over time. The richer the person's history of reinforcement, the more likely it is that he or she will have a "well-developed, interesting personality." In Skinner's approach, no specific stages of development are assumed.

We are considered by Skinner to be behavior emitters, and what we become is determined primarily by the outcomes that our behaviors have. Some behaviors will increase in frequency, whereas others will remain relatively stable, decrease in frequency, or completely disappear, depending on their consequences.

ROGERS stresses the possibility of continual growth and fulfillment. Unfavorable circumstances (such as conditional love) may cramp development and cause maladaptive behaviors, but, if given the chance (for example, through exposure to unconditional positive regard and empathic understanding), most persons can reestablish their actualization tendencies. No specific stages are posited, and humans are capable, through awareness and sound choices, of an ever-upward spiraling in their development.

According to Rogers, a personality that is flexible and able to adapt to the requirements of new situations will result when an individual experiences unconditional positive regard. A relatively static and defensive personality is likely to result if conditional (rather than unconditional) positive regard is experienced to a significant degree.

Views of Maladjustment and Therapy

FREUD saw neurosis as an internally rooted problem brought about primarily by conflicts between unconscious desires and the demands of society. Civilized humans suffer emotional conflicts and tensions that have all sorts of behavioral manifestations. The inner dynamics of the person are extremely important; initially these dynamics result from instinctive impulses, but the outer world also has its effects and greatly complicates the inner workings. For example, when certain experiences are repressed, this material, plus the instinctive impulses, can generate various disturbances. Psychoanalytic therapy attempts to get at the unconscious sources of problems—that is, to reveal them and work them through so that individuals can adapt realistically to their inner impulses and to their environments.

SKINNER stresses environmental causes of maladaptive behavior. Excessive punishment or aversive control, as well as the reinforcement of undesirable behaviors, can create individuals labeled by others as "neurotic" or "psychotic." Skinner does not view such persons as having unconscious conflicts, distorted self-concepts, or some other "inner problem." He believes that it is inefficient to speculate about, or to try to deal with, hypothetical inner states; it is best to stay at the behavioral level, where objective analyses can take place.

Since observable behaviors are emphasized, and maladaptive behaviors are considered to result from aversive conditions or poorly controlled or misapplied reinforcements, Skinner's recommendations for "therapy" involve providing opportunities for alternative, adaptive behaviors that can be shaped and maintained through reinforcement, the extinction of undesirable behaviors, and better control of the contingencies of reinforcement operating in the individual's life.

ROGERS' theory suggests that maladaptive feelings and behaviors can be traced to the interruption, sidetracking, or stunting of actualization processes. Conditional positive regard inhibits or distorts normal growth and self-development. Since Rogers considers human nature to be primarily positive (oriented toward intimate and accurate awareness of one's experiencing and toward good relationships with others), people will develop serious problems in how they feel or behave only if their basic nature is corrupted by social influences.

Therapy involves creating an atmosphere of acceptance, empathic understanding, and genuineness that alleviates the need for defensiveness and allows the exploration of all feelings and other inner experiencing. There is a much greater emphasis on conscious capacities in client-centered therapy than in Freudian therapy; that is, Rogers tends to accept what the client says in the here-and-now, and he has a great deal of confidence in human powers of self-discovery if a warm, accepting atmosphere exists. Rogers feels that it is best not to interpret hidden meanings in what clients say but rather to allow them to revise their statements as therapy proceeds so that they will come closer and closer to expressing their real experiencing. The responsibility is on the client to accurately understand and express himself or herself, and this ability increases during therapy.

A great deal of emphasis is placed on the client's developing freedom of choice, and Rogers is opposed to viewing the person in therapy as an "object" to be changed by the therapist. Behaviorists are sometimes accused—although probably seldom with justification—of treating persons as objects to be controlled or manipulated. It has also been suggested that orthodox Freudian analysts impose their interpretations on their patients, rather than allowing therapy to be an open and free-flowing process. There are various pro and con arguments on the issue of the extent to which a patient has the ability to determine the therapeutic process, and Rogers' view represents the "client-determined" end of the continuum. Even here, however, the therapist is influencing the client by establishing a particular therapeutic "climate."

Views of Society's Role

FREUD believed that there is continual conflict between human nature and civilization. Instincts promoting sex and aggression are not easily reconciled with the amenities demanded by society. By providing numerous possibilities for sublimation, however, society can ease this conflict. It is the task of parents, educators, and other agents of the culture to inhibit basic human drives to some extent, but constructive outlets should also be offered. Society is often too restrictive; it should make compromises possible by providing constructive channels for the use of instinctive energies. Civilization survives and grows through sexual and aggressive drives that are partially inhibited and partially sublimated.

SKINNER emphasizes that society, since it *does* control the behaviors of its members (whether or not this is acknowledged openly), needs to take seriously its responsibilities. He believes that the many problems of human conduct are too serious and complex to leave to chance or to antiquated and ill-formed concepts of freedom and dignity. He suggests that those who continually espouse the values of freedom and dignity generally miss the point that human behavior is always affected by environmental factors; they confuse the issue by assuming that humans can somehow operate outside the cause-and-effect concepts of conditioning. Also, in their attempts to avoid aversive control, they often resist *any* form of control; this causes them to overlook the benefits of systematically applied positive reinforcement.

The primary role of society in Skinner's view is to set up planned, systematic contingencies of reinforcement that will maximize desirable behaviors. Since humans are malleable, behavioral engineering is the crux of the matter. Environmental control is needed to foster behaviors that are both personally and socially advantageous (for example, behaviors that are "peaceful," "cooperative," and "considerate"), and programs should be instituted to shape and maintain these behaviors. Also, techniques that tend to produce undesirable problem behaviors should be done away with; for example, the use of punishment and aversive control should be avoided.

ROGERS sees society as generally too restrictive and static. Humans are destined at birth to grow and flourish as individuals and as social beings, but parents, teachers, employers, and so on upset this destiny by imposing established values and forcing adherence to them. If Rogers' views prevailed, society's institutions (the home, schools, government, and so on) would become processes rather than rigid and static structures. In his opinion, human potential for actualization is great, and it cannot be known now what humans will be in the future if this potential is developed. Therefore, society should allow freedom for experimentation in alternative life-styles and for creative outlets of all types; also, very importantly, society should allow failures to occur without condemnation. Humans are engaged in a struggle "to be and to become," and society should maintain flexibility and avoid censuring different attempts to achieve growth and fulfillment.

Views on the Study of Human Behavior

FREUD favored an inductive-type approach to theory development. He tied together various observations in order to form general concepts (rather than first constructing an elaborate theory from which to draw specific assumptions). These concepts were then refined or altered as he continued to treat his patients, to investigate his own unconscious, to study literature, and to observe social events. He was not experimentally oriented, and he didn't collect quantitative data; instead, his data were qualitative and subject to interpretation. He concentrated heavily on the intensive study of individual therapy cases, attempting to verify his ideas by noting consistencies and inconsistencies relating to those ideas.

Freud advocated an openness concerning definitions of concepts, suggesting that definitions be changed if observations provide new information. This attitude is reflected in his writings during the many years in which he was active in developing psychoanalytic theory. (In fact, the reader who is unaware of Freud's tendency to assign somewhat different meanings to terms at different times is apt to be led astray in attempts to understand Freudian psychology.)

From what has just been said, it should not be thought that Freud changed his ideas quickly and easily. He often showed a reluctance to give up a formulation once it had been developed and did not always follow his own advice about being open to modifications. However, the history of psychoanalytic theory shows that, in the long run, he did make substantial changes.

SKINNER emphasizes the experimental method of gaining information about behavior. He advocates precise determinations of *functional relations* (or, in less formal terms, "cause-and-effect connections") between independent and dependent variables. An *independent variable* is a factor that is varied systematically in order to study its effects on some specified behavior, which is referred to as the *dependent variable.* For example, the length of time between reinforcers might be varied (this would be the independent variable) in order to study the effects of these variations on a pigeon's key-pecking behavior (a dependent variable). With humans, the dependent variable might be behavior such as job or academic performance.

In short, Skinner feels that it is of primary importance to investigate the observable factors of which behavior is a function. Experimental conditions provide the means for careful manipulations of various factors and for the accurate quantitative measurement of resulting behaviors.

The Skinner box provides a way of objectively studying the behavior of lower animals. Findings from such studies allow the formation of basic concepts that can then be tested at the human level. Methods for precise control and measurement are also applicable to the study of human behavior. For example, if the effectiveness of a change in rein-forcement contingencies is to be studied, *baseline data* are first col-lected. Baseline data allow the comparison of the frequency of partic-ular behaviors *before* the change is introduced with the frequency of these behaviors *after* the change has been made.

Skinner is not "theoretical" in the typical sense of that word. He is opposed to the use of abstract concepts and formal hypothesis-testing. He believes that research can be performed effectively without a theory. In fact, he feels that theories can distract from the basic goal of finding out what causes what, because they may misrepresent the basic facts, give the illusion that more is known than actually is, and result in the persistent use of ineffective methods. In general, Skinner takes the position that theory-testing is a waste of time and that psychologists should concern themselves with collecting data and relating these data to observable variables. He has suggested that there is a use for "theory" if that term indicates a formal representation of data that have already been collected and analyzed; in other words, Skinner does acknowledge the need for tying together significant findings in a meaningful way— once these findings have been obtained. This descriptive approach dif-fers from using a relatively abstract theory from which hypotheses are formulated and tested, a practice commonly engaged in by psycholog-ical researchers but frowned on by Skinner.

Like Freud, Skinner concentrated heavily on the study of individual cases, although with Skinner the "individuals" were most frequently rats or pigeons in experimental situations rather than humans in ther-apy situations (in more recent years, however, other behaviorists have done many studies with humans in a variety of situations). Skinner believes that a science of behavior should be able to control, with exact-ness, the behavior of each individual organism and should not be sat-isfied with statements about what occurs "on the average." He has performed detailed analyses of environmental factors that cause spe-cific changes in the behaviors of individual organisms, and in this way he has developed precise behavioral concepts.

Although Freud's work involved the intensive study of individual sub-jects, he did not seem convinced that precise statements about behav-ior are possible; Freud's approach was not designed to make psychology an exact science. Also, of course, Freud's data were qualitative, whereas Skinner's basic data are quantitative.

ROGERS has indicated that objective, quantitative approaches to the study of human behavior (such as that used by Skinner) are important means of obtaining knowledge. However, he also places great emphasis on subjective knowledge (knowing oneself) and on empathic, or inter-personal, phenomenological knowledge (understanding the subjective states of others). He feels that it is necessary to pursue all of these avenues—*objective, subjective,* and *empathic.* Rogers is inclusive, rather than exclusive, in his recommendations about methods for studying humans and believes that an adequate behavioral science depends on the interweaving of these three ways of knowing. To him, there is no absolutely certain path to "true" scientific knowledge; different meth-ods must be used in an interrelated fashion to allow more complete understanding of human behavior.

Although stressing the importance of all three of the above ways of knowing, Rogers has proposed that the most basic is subjective know-ing. He feels that science always begins from internal frames of refer-ence; that is, inner subjective experiencing provides the basic material from which consciously stated hypotheses are formed. He believes that even strict behaviorists, who revere objective and quantitative scien-tific techniques, start out with feelings and hunches (inner subjective experiences) that carry them forward along certain lines of research. Rogers has suggested that creative inner hypotheses emerge from indi-vidual experiencing, that these hypotheses are then checked through further experiencing, and that eventually they may reach the stage of formally stated concepts that can be tested by objective scientific methods.

As Rogers notes, even when hypotheses are tested objectively, the objective evidence is fitted to subjective experiencing; if it doesn't fit right, it may be evaluated much more critically than if it does fit right. He has used the research on extrasensory perception as an example (see Rogers' article in Wann's *Behaviorism and Phenomenology,* 1964, p. 114, which was referenced at the end of Chapter 4). Even though there is some evidence to indicate the possibility of ESP, many psy-chologists reject it strongly because it does not fit their subjective expec-tancies. In brief, Rogers feels that both subjectivity and objectivity are aspects of the scientific process and that this fact must be given attention.

In Rogers' view, Freud was too wrapped up in his notions of our unconscious and irrational qualities, and radical behaviorists concen-trate too much on studying humans as objects. Rogers' recommenda-tions involve looking at humans more as conscious and rational beings and attempting to understand their subjective experiencing. Rogers has used research data to support some of his contentions about human behavior, but he does not put these data on a pedestal of special sci-entific respectability. He believes that there is such a thing as "the whole person," and he sees the value of a variety of means of attempting to understand individuals.

Recently, Rogers has reiterated his opinion that psychologists typi-cally adhere too rigidly to traditional and confining research methods and statistical designs.[1] Instead of being so concerned about the use of particular methods and designs, their emphasis should be on ensuring that they themselves are (1) well informed but open minded, (2) able to be "in-dwelling"—that is, able to enter the inner world of subjects' experiencing while also maintaining objectivity, (3) able to avoid premature or preconceived conclusions, and (4) able to express findings in a clear, well-organized manner.

Views on a Vital Social Problem: Destructive Aggression

FREUD stressed, with much concern, our propensity for destruction. He believed that this tendency is inherent in human nature as an outgrowth of the death instinct. For example, in a 1932 letter to Albert Einstein, Freud expressed the belief that wars can be attributed to aggressive impulses that can never be gotten rid of completely. He suggested that these aggressive impulses may, however, be brought under at least partial control through the establishment of emotional ties among people (for example, shared interests cause identifications among people, or a "community of feeling") and through the strengthening of humans' conscious reasoning and controlling functions. In addition, Freudian theory suggests that aggressive impulses can sometimes be redirected into socially constructive activities (that is, they can be sublimated) and that certain inhibitions against aggression (such as moral values) can be developed during the socialization process. Despite these possible means of controlling innate destructive tendencies, Freud's writings generally seem to be pessimistic about civilization's ability to cope effectively with the problem of aggression.

SKINNER suggests that an innate component may be involved in certain types of aggressive responses (for example, hitting or biting when physically attacked) as a result of the possible contribution of these responses to the survival of the species during evolutionary history. However, the main thrust of his explanation for harmful, destructive behaviors relies on environmental factors, such as past and present contingencies of reinforcement. For example, if aggressive behavior results in "getting what you want," then you will tend to repeat that type of behavior.

According to Skinnerian thought, if the world could be changed so that there were no payoff for destructively aggressive behaviors, they would be drastically reduced in frequency. The "payoff" might involve removing something aversive, such as a threat from another person,

---

[1]See *APA Monitor*, May 1985, p. 16.

or obtaining something positive. The former is negative reinforcement, and the latter is positive reinforcement. A reduction of harmfully aggressive behavior requires a change in conditions that negatively and positively reinforce such behavior.

ROGERS' theory suggests that harmful or unreasonable aggression is most likely to be shown by persons who aren't fully functioning. Persons who are more fully functioning (that is, those who are more in touch with their deep inner experiencing and who have clearer perspectives on the world around them) are not likely to be destructively aggressive. Such individuals are highly social beings who want harmonious interpersonal relationships; if they do engage in aggression, it is likely to be realistically appropriate—that is, justified and suitable.

Rogers emphasizes human abilities to be rational and to be able to make appropriate responses to situations. These abilities will supposedly develop naturally if the proper conditions exist (for example, unconditional positive regard). Therefore, a solution offered by Rogers for the problem of human destructiveness is the creation of conditions that allow fulfillment of basic human potentialities. (It is particularly interesting to reflect on the differences between Freud's and Rogers' thinking about basic human nature when considering the problem of destructive aggression.)

Rogers versus Skinner
on Controlling Human Behavior

An article entitled "Some Issues Concerning the Control of Human Behavior" was published in the November 30, 1956, issue of *Science*. The material was from a symposium held at the annual meeting of the American Psychological Association, during which Rogers and Skinner presented their respective views. We will consider briefly some of their differences.

Skinner emphasizes that human behavior *is* controlled. He believes that this is an inescapable fact that cannot be avoided. According to him, each person is involved in both controlling and being controlled; a scientific, experimental analysis of behavior can provide data to elucidate these processes of control and can be used to improve areas of human functioning such as personal control, education, and government. Skinner suggests that traditional ways of looking at behavior, which often assign responsibility to forces *within* individuals rather than to environmental factors, impede progress in improving the human situation. He advocates letting science lead the way by using its objective, experimentally derived techniques (such as the application of positive reinforcement) to develop more productive and socially beneficial behaviors.

Rogers' main reservation with regard to Skinner's proposals is the question of what purposes or values should guide the use of control. Also, he feels that Skinner does not give adequate attention to the problem of power and to matters such as who will be controlled, who will do the controlling, and what kind of control will be utilized.

Rogers and Skinner both agree that the behavioral sciences have made significant progress in predicting and controlling behavior. They differ sharply, however, in their views of how to proceed with this knowledge and in their views about the limitations of science. Rogers believes that there are subjective value choices that *must* be made outside the scientific endeavor. In other words, he suggests that the goals of science are necessarily established subjectively and that these goals guide the scientist and those who use scientific findings. To Rogers, the role of these subjective value judgments cannot be dismissed; such values *are* chosen, and they *do* dictate scientific pursuits by determining the problems to be investigated, the methods to be used, the acceptability and application of the findings, and so on. Science itself cannot determine its own progress; this responsibility, according to Rogers, rests with persons who make choices and decisions. Furthermore, he argues that subjective judgments must be made about the use of scientific findings in the critical and sensitive area of behavior control.

In response, Skinner disagrees that subjective, inner choices have to be considered in relation to science. Arguing along lines that are familiar in his reasoning, Skinner suggests that "choices" of goals and values do not take place in some realm removed from external, environmental circumstances. He warns that an emphasis on the importance of human subjectivity distracts from the intelligent use of scientific findings to better the world in which we live. The major points in Skinner's presentation are that: (1) an objective science of behavior can and should be applied to correct the ills of society and the problem behaviors of individuals; (2) the effects of attempts to control behavior can be observed, and changes can be made in those attempts that do not promote cultural survival; and (3) references to subjective value choices simply cloud the issue by drawing attention away from the effects of the environment on behavior.

The issues raised during the symposium were not settled at that time, nor have they been settled yet. Rogers consistently has argued for the importance of individual feelings, thoughts, and other inner experiences; to him, these experiences are central, and science must include them. Objective scientific methods have their places too, according to Rogers, but they should be considered primarily as means of aiding personal growth and fulfillment. He feels that human development is a fluid process and that end states are unpredictable if adequate opportunities for actualization are available; therefore, concepts of science should also be in a continual state of change to meet newly arising human needs and wants.

Skinner, on the other hand, believes that an objective science of behavior should be in the forefront, providing the data needed for maximizing the conditions for human survival. He indicates that, like it or not, external factors do operate on individuals and do determine their behaviors. In his view, the best way to deal with this fact is to investigate as fully as possible the various ways in which we control others and are ourselves controlled; experimental analyses of behavior provide this information. If we accept the fact of control, and gain as much scientific information about it as possible, we can plan intelligently. The environment can be structured in the best ways to produce "healthy, happy, secure, productive, and creative people" (these are the types of behaviors Skinner suggests would result if his behavioral approach were put into effect).

■   CRITICISMS   ■

Criticisms have been leveled at each of the three approaches we have been discussing. Followers of each approach, of course, tend to make certain negative evaluations of the others. Also, interested "outsiders," who have no particular vested interest, have criticized various points. Although occasionally someone argues for the total rejection of one or another of these approaches, such arguments seem somewhat premature. Presently, each view has something to contribute; more study, however, will likely result in the development of increasingly sophisticated concepts of human behavior that may firmly displace certain existing ideas.

What follows are some of the common criticisms made of each approach. I have tried to avoid being highly technical by sticking to fairly major, general types of criticisms.

Criticisms of Freud

Freud was not greatly concerned about the empirical specificity of his terms and concepts. Therefore, his theory is difficult to validate. For example, how can the notion of the death instinct be put to a reasonably rigorous test? It can be inferred from various verbal statements or from other behaviors, but these are subject to many alternative interpretations. For example, suicide or destructively aggressive behavior can be explained in various ways that have nothing to do with a death instinct. Vague constructs are prevalent in Freud's theory: the Oedipus complex, libido, fixation, castration anxiety, and so on. These concepts are stimulating, but they are extremely difficult to operationalize (that is, they lack the concrete specificity necessary for applying the methods of objective science).

Freud pieced together many bits of information from his own behavior, the behavior of his patients, and events in the world at large in order to develop his many notions. Was he accurate in his observations? Was he able to be objective enough to avoid his own biases? Were his interpretations correct? These and other questions can and should be asked. In the absence of more rigorous, experimental-type evidence, it is difficult to accept many of Freud's ideas as having proven validity. This should not be interpreted to mean that Freud's ideas have never been tested experimentally.[2] There have been various attempts, but many are inconclusive because of questionable *operational definitions* (an operational definition involves the translation of an abstract concept into specific terms so that the concept can be manipulated or measured objectively).

The persons Freud studied while developing his theory constituted a fairly restricted sample. In other words, the cultural and socioeconomic range of his patients was rather limited, and this fact perhaps limits the general applicability of his ideas. Also, he relied heavily on observations of neurotic persons (his patients) in forming his theory. Can a theory developed largely on the basis of observations of a limited group of neurotic persons be considered a valid theory of human behavior? Abraham Maslow, a noted humanistic psychologist, felt strongly that such theories are necessarily incomplete. He believed that different assumptions are needed to explain the behavior of better-functioning persons. This may or may not be true. Again, it is very difficult to put Freud's theory to a thorough test to determine its generality.

A number of criticisms have been made concerning Freud's methods of accumulating evidence to build and support his theory. He did not keep a verbatim record of therapy sessions (if he had, it might have hindered the therapeutic process); rather, he tended to rely on his memory in making notes hours later. Certainly this procedure could have allowed omissions and distortions to creep into his accounts of the therapeutic process. Furthermore, Freud has been faulted for accepting his patients' verbalizations without trying to check them out adequately with outside sources such as records or interviews with relatives. He may not have had the time for outside investigations, but the lack of such supportive data does decrease the credibility of his assumptions. An additional criticism is that he was not systematic in

[2]For surveys and analyses of studies of Freud's ideas, see Seymour Fisher's and Roger P. Greenberg's *The Scientific Credibility of Freud's Theories and Therapy* (New York: Basic Books, 1977) and Paul Kline's *Fact and Fantasy in Freudian Theory*, 2nd ed. (London: Methuen, 1981). For a discussion of how psychoanalytic research might be improved, see Marshall Edelson's *Hypothesis and Evidence in Psychoanalysis* (Chicago: University of Chicago Press, 1984).

presenting the steps by which he arrived at certain conclusions. It is next to impossible for another person to repeat the processes Freud went through in deriving and attempting to substantiate his theoretical concepts.

An objection often made about psychoanalytic theory is that it explains too much too easily. For example, persons who engage in a great deal of sexual behavior are supposedly expressing their instinctual impulses; persons who do not display much sexual behavior may be said to be inhibited; persons who show a moderate amount of sexual interest are assumed to have worked out a compromise between their sexual impulses and their inhibitions. No matter what the case may be, Freudian theory is ready with an explanation. A problem arises, however, in trying to determine which behavior is the most likely under a given set of conditions. It is not enough to have a possible explanation; a strong theory should be able to state when and how a particular outcome will occur, and psychoanalysis does this only in a very general and often confusing way.

As a last-but-not-least criticism, Freud's model of personality as an energy system totally propelled by instincts can be seriously questioned. It certainly seems doubtful that *all* human behavior can be traced to sexual and aggressive drives that demand release in one form or another. This tension-reduction view of human activity (that is, that all behavior stems from the need to reduce inner tensions) is contradicted by research indicating that humans and lower animals often seek, rather than avoid, stimulation. Even casual observations of children at play seem to bear out the idea that "curiosity" is prevalent and that novel experiences are sought. These data from research and observations cannot be easily explained from the Freudian point of view, which stresses human strivings to achieve a state in which tension is absent.

Criticisms of Skinner

Skinner often stresses the importance of collecting objective, scientific data and of basing one's assumptions on this type of evidence. However, there are times when Skinner himself goes far beyond his experimental findings to make recommendations on a grand scale. He has been accused of doing so in *Beyond Freedom and Dignity*, in which he makes certain assumptions and proposals concerning behavior at the societal level. Is this attempt justified? On the basis of animal and human research that has focused on the behavior of *individual* organisms (mainly in highly controlled situations), can he validly deal with problems of enormously greater magnitude, such as the running of a whole society? Is Skinner presumptuous in his reasoning? It certainly is true that he has uncovered, and supported with much data, certain basic concepts of behavior, which have proven to be quite effective for use in mental institutions, educational programs, business and industrial settings, and so on. But are they really sufficient to cope fully with very complex social problems? These types of questions cannot be answered adequately at this time. It may be that Skinner's relatively simple behavioral concepts do apply to the whole range of human activities, but not many persons are now willing to accept that assumption.

While strongly advocating that society operate on the basis of a scientific approach, using behavioral technology to solve its problems, Skinner has not been very specific about how this broad social change could occur. Who will exert the power to set up certain contingencies of reinforcement, and who will determine which behaviors are to be reinforced? He has addressed these issues, but in such a way that the answers sometimes seem philosophical rather than practical. He doesn't satisfy those who are skeptical about the possibilities of social change based on positive reinforcement. Perhaps the best answer he has given is that those who already are in positions of influence—teachers, parents, work supervisors, government officials, and so on—are the ones who can apply behavioral techniques. How this could occur on a society-wide scale, and which specific behaviors would be reinforced if society as a whole were involved, are more difficult questions.

Skinner has been criticized by humanistic psychologists and others who say that his ideas directly or indirectly encourage treating persons as objects to be manipulated. It's easy to see how his emphasis on behavior control might be considered dehumanizing. His defenders, however, indicate that he provides effective techniques that can be used by individuals themselves to change their own behaviors. Also, knowledge of his approach allows a degree of countercontrol; that is, the controllers can be controlled. Still, Skinner perhaps has not been sufficiently clear in pointing out the line between *use* and *misuse* of his behavioral concepts.

Another sticky question that can be asked of Skinner is: if we are all controlled by our environments, and if we have no free choice, how can we "decide" to follow his recommendations and put his suggested programs into effect? According to his behavioral approach, there is no such thing as free choice; therefore, it seems inappropriate for him to suggest that we "accept" his proposals. Skinner has at times responded to questions of this type, but his answers don't seem fully satisfying (for example, see pages 246–248 in *About Behaviorism*). They leave the lingering feeling that he is asking us to do something that is apparently in violation of his approach, and a thorough understanding of radical behaviorism is necessary in order to resolve that feeling. The basic notion is that the behavior of each of us (including Skinner) is controlled by our environmental experiences. This holds whether one is in the position of proposing the acceptance of behaviorism (as Skinner is) or of "accepting" that proposal (as his readers are). "Acceptance," then, is not a freely chosen alternative; if one accepts Skinnerian psychology, it is because of one's history of reinforcement and presently existing circumstances. (For example, if readers have been reinforced in the past for following advice in books, they may follow the advice given in Skinner's books; in Skinner's terms, they would be engaging in "rule-governed behavior.") Many critics of Skinner find great difficulty with this type of explanation, which is based on his completely deterministic view of human behavior.

As stated previously, Skinnerian concepts have been used quite effectively in various therapeutic, educational, business, and industrial settings. However, there sometimes are shortcomings even when environments within such settings are carefully controlled. Behavioral engineering has often brought about impressive results, but it has not always been as effective as hoped. How can results that are short of the mark be explained? If psychotic or neurotic behaviors are improved, but not to the point at which the individual can function "normally," what is being neglected? If a child learns more than usual when exposed to a teaching machine, but still is unable to completely master the subject, what is wrong? Perhaps cases in which success falls short of expectations can be explained by oversights on the part of the person or persons responsible for the behavioral-engineering program; that is, certain significant environmental factors might have been overlooked or not adequately controlled. However, it is also possible that there is more to behavior than meets the radical behaviorist's eye; maybe additional or more complex principles are operating. The answer awaits more extensive and detailed study.

Skinner's position on punishment is another commonly criticized point. He has often asserted that punishment has detrimental effects and that it does not permanently eliminate unwanted behaviors. Although these views might be taken as signs of his humanism, they are scientifically questionable. At least under certain conditions, punishment does seem to be effective in controlling behavior and does not seem to have long-lasting negative effects. Punishments sometimes curtail undesirable behaviors so that alternative, desirable behaviors can be shaped with positive reinforcers. Of course, in such cases the alternatives must be available; simply applying punishment is not likely to produce desirable outcomes. Fairly severe electric shocks have been used on autistic, self-mutilating children to stop them from injuring themselves. These children hit or bite themselves, bang their heads against hard objects, and harm themselves in other ways. By shocking them when they engage in such behaviors, behavior modifiers have successfully stopped this self-abuse; once this behavior is prevented, positive behaviors can then be shaped. (For a brief article on the positive uses of punishment, see D. M. Baer's "Let's Take Another Look at

Punishment," in *Psychology Today*, October 1971.) It should not be inferred from what has just been said that punishment is more desirable than positive reinforcement as a general technique of control; the point is simply that Skinner has perhaps been overly zealous in his rejection of punishment as an effective behavior-control technique.

Critics also have pointed to the weaknesses of Skinner's explanations of novel behaviors, such as unique verbal expressions, creative problem-solving approaches, and artistic accomplishments. It's true that his explanations seem strained. However, it must be asked whether the alternative explanations are any better. Skinner acknowledges that radical behaviorism cannot be expected, at this time, to provide fully adequate accounts of all complex behaviors.

Criticisms of Rogers

Rogers has been accused of practicing naïve phenomenology by accepting at face value what his clients say. A large amount of psychological evidence indicates that it is extremely difficult for a person to understand and express adequately "real" feelings or thoughts. Even though Rogers has listened carefully to his clients in order to understand their inner experiencing, it still may be that he has not discovered the most basic determinants of human functioning. Since the verbalizations of his clients have been a major source of data for Rogers' theoretical assumptions, it is important to question the reliability and validity of these data. Is it possible to get a satisfactorily complete picture of individuals by simply listening to them?

It must be said that Rogers is aware of the problems of his phenomenology, and he has advocated and even employed other techniques (such as the *Q*-sort) to test and support his theory. The fact remains, however, that he has been affected strongly by clinical experiences during which he has attempted to listen with care and empathy to his clients. Have they revealed their "true selves"—that is, the critical aspects of human experiencing? The possibility exists that conscious or unconscious distortions may have been present in their statements.

Another kind of naïveté of which Rogers has been accused concerns his view of basic human nature. If humans are inherently good, why have they made such a mess of things? Perhaps Rogerian theory places too much emphasis on our "better side." It is easy to see how a person can become "bad" if he or she has been raised under severe circumstances of conditional positive regard. But how did we *initially* get so far off the track, so that we now raise generation after generation of inadequately functioning individuals?

Also, what is the explanation when a child raised with love and freedom turns out to be a selfish, manipulative, and generally maladjusted adult? (Rogers might say that unconditional positive regard was more apparent than real in such a case.) On the other side of this coin, how about the child who is made to adhere to a rigid code of ethics and behavior and who nevertheless develops into an empathic, creative, and sociable adult? Of course, theories of human behavior cannot be expected at this point in psychological history to be perfect—there are exceptions to the rules established by any existing theory. However, attention to these exceptions can help to ensure a proper perspective on the general validity of various theories.

Rogers assumes that we have a built-in mechanism that allows us, if we remain in tune with it, to make the appropriate moves in our lives. This organismic valuing process will supposedly direct us to wise decisions and behaviors. What firm evidence is there for an innate mechanism that helps us make the right choices? Perhaps a more important question is this: how can the operation of the organismic valuing process be separated from the effects of learned cultural values? We begin to learn at birth—that's obvious. Can all these subtle, as well as direct, learnings be separated from some supposedly innate process? Where can the line (if any) be drawn between "learned" and "natural"?

A criticism leveled by psychoanalysts against Rogers is that he gives too little attention to unconscious processes. He does, of course, refer to inadequately symbolized experiences (experiences of which the person is not fully conscious), but his view is that the individual can become aware of these experiences if unconditional positive regard, empathy, and genuineness exist. Psychoanalysts reject this position, saying that analytic interpretations and the "working through" of transferences are necessary for understanding the unconscious. Also, psychoanalysis holds that certain portions of the personality will always remain at the unconscious level.

Radical behaviorists see Rogers' theory as being based on observations under uncontrolled conditions. In other words, they believe that much of what he claims to be the result of unconditional positive regard is actually due to unspecified contingencies of reinforcement. To Skinner, there is no such thing as giving a person the freedom to behave as he or she wishes; contingencies of reinforcement are always in operation. Therefore, to Skinner and others of his persuasion, Rogers is fooling himself into thinking that his clients develop freedom of choice as therapy progresses; if client-centered therapists do not actively apply reinforcers, the client's behavior will be affected by other reinforcements, such as those existing outside the therapy situation.

It may be that client-centered therapists, despite themselves, bring about changes in the client's behaviors through inadvertent, subtle reinforcements (for example, nodding their heads or changing their facial expressions when clients speak about "interesting" things and remaining more passive when clients speak about "uninteresting" things). The client's behavioral changes may then cause other persons to react to him or her differently in everyday life (that is, different contingencies of reinforcement go into operation). This type of process could, in the long run, result in significant changes that the client-centered therapist would attribute to unconditional positive regard, empathy, and genuineness.

As a final comment, certain of Rogers' concepts are very broad and vague. For example, "organismic experiencing" includes so much that it comes dangerously close to being meaningless. The terms "self-concept" and "fully functioning" are also so inclusive that they almost defy comprehension. Perhaps more specific subclassifications within these general concepts would help. Also, Rogers sometimes attempts to convey ideas that he admits he cannot explain precisely and for which there is little available research evidence. Perhaps in these cases the only reader he touches is the one who already agrees with him; the skeptic may not be able to relate adequately or appropriately to Rogers' statements. In other words, it may be that one has to be a "believer" already in order to understand some of Rogers' theoretical notions.

■   CONCLUDING COMMENTS   ■

Some General Comments

The criticisms made in the previous section should not be disheartening. Only if perfection were expected (and this expectation is premature if psychology's relatively brief history is considered) would there be cause for discouragement concerning the weaknesses in these three major approaches. Each view has something of interest to offer to those who want to understand their own behavior and the behavior of others. Also—and very importantly—each view is serving as a spur to research in psychology and other behavioral sciences. The ideas of Freud, Skinner, and Rogers are sufficiently stimulating to produce researchers of each persuasion who attempt to support their adopted point of view; perhaps the best way for science to progress is to have dedicated researchers pursue different avenues of thought with vigor and determination. In the future, when various dead ends have been reached and alternative paths have been relatively successful, there may be a weeding out, a slimming down, a tying in, and so on, so that as a result facets of each theory will become integrated into a thorough understanding of human behavior.

For the present, each theorist can be admired for his contributions. Freud focused on many aspects of human functioning that typically receive little systematic attention: irrational fears, fantasies, dreams, sexual conflicts, psychosomatic disorders, childhood neuroses, and so on. His ideas are broad in their coverage and stimulating in their content. Skinner has developed concepts that have wide practical applicability, and his emphasis on the environment's effects on behavior helps to ensure that due consideration is given to these "outside" determinants. Rogers has helped to sustain and guide interest in the concept of "self," which puts an emphasis on unique human qualities. Also, he often has reminded psychologists and others that there is no single, sure road to "truth" and that the full range of human abilities— subjective, empathic, and objective—can be applied in the pursuit of knowledge.

Some Personal Comments

Aside from their scientific value, and in terms of personal philosophies of life, of what use are these different views? On this point each person must speak for himself or herself. I will try to state some of their meanings for me.

Freud makes me ask myself "Do I really know *why* I'm doing what I'm doing?" He causes me to question my motives and also to try to reduce my possible blindness to obnoxious characteristics, prejudices, or biases that I might have. The idea of "defense mechanisms" has always been fascinating to me. Freud saw these mechanisms as operating unconsciously, but I believe that sometimes we can recognize and change our own defensive behaviors.

Also, it seems to me that the notion of defense mechanisms is valuable in dealing with other people. Caution must always be exerted in applying the term "defensive" to another's behavior, and I would urge that this practice be avoided in general. The importance of the idea of defensiveness in interpersonal (and intergroup) relations is *not* in labeling the behaviors of others but in trying to react reasonably to those behaviors. I sometimes have found that my reactions to others have changed for the better (occasionally this has meant avoiding someone who is extremely hard to get along with) when I have seen clearly that they are operating defensively. This awareness can effectively prevent certain everyday conflicts.

Although I believe that defensiveness is an important and useful psychoanalytic concept, I also believe that certain other Freudian concepts and notions are totally (or almost totally) off base. A prime example is the idea that destructive aggression is instinctive. Whereas an instinctive component may be involved in some aggressive acts (for example, when we strike out at someone who is inflicting pain on us), I believe that aggression primarily is *learned* behavior. Aggressive persons often are modeling (imitating) the aggressive acts of others (parents, friends, movie and TV heroes, and so on) and/or have been, or are being, reinforced for such behavior. Environmental factors, such as stressful or highly competitive situations, can trigger learned aggression. Another factor in some cases is brain pathology; a brain that is malfunctioning because of inherited or acquired damage may not be able to regulate behavior adequately. Blood chemistry also seems to play a role in aggression; certain hormonal changes appear to affect the occurrence of aggressive behaviors.

I see no reason to hold to Freud's motivational theory of instincts, even if we were to talk about sex rather than aggression. Sexual behavior, as well as aggressive behavior, is largely under the control of environmental conditions. The "strength" of the so-called sexual drive is influenced by past reinforcing and/or punishing sexual experiences, the availability of sexual partners, amount of deprivation, and so on. Such factors are more useful for explaining human behavior than is the notion of a "basic sexual drive."

With regard to *Skinner,* he has made an extremely important contribution by pointing repeatedly to the environment's effects on behavior. Though his concepts may fall short of providing an adequate account of the whole range of human functioning, I believe that they have a potential that is far from being fully realized at this time. He has opened the door to the investigation of all the influences that our physical and social environments have on our behaviors, and the prospects are exciting. His approach allows the systematic study of the ways in which the environment acts on the genetic endowment of individuals to select certain behaviors. By using the obtainable information, we can improve ourselves and society.

Skinner draws attention to an obviously important aspect of human life: reinforcement. It is significant for controlling our own behaviors, raising children, improving education, getting along with others, and most other activities. Reinforcement seems so simple that we often ignore it. Many behaviors have become more understandable when I have focused on the positive and negative reinforcers affecting me and others. Also, many social problems—delinquency, criminal activities, school failures, violence, and so on—seem to stem at least partially from the lack of positive reinforcements for "desirable" behavior and the concurrent immediate reinforcement for "undesirable" behavior.

The deprived person who successfully steals is reinforced right away; if the only alternative is to wait endlessly to save money while doing a menial (perhaps even degrading) job, then the immediate reinforcement for stealing may control behavior. I don't think that all problem behaviors can be explained this simply (nor does Skinner), but sometimes we overlook the obvious. Another example is violent, destructive behavior. The person who behaves violently may have no other means of escaping from punishment or aversive conditions, or this may be the only way that positive reinforcement can be obtained.

Reinforcement can be personally relevant also. In my own life, I've observed changes in my behavior as contingencies of reinforcement changed. It's sometimes possible to set up effective contingencies that help ensure productive activity. For myself, simple devices often have yielded big gains. When I plan to do a great deal of writing (or studying or reading) over a prolonged period (weeks or months), I try to set up a schedule that allows reinforcement after a number of hours of concentrated effort each day. It seems that, if I regularly quit working after a certain number of hours and spend the rest of the day doing something enjoyable, I am better able to keep up the effort on a day-after-day basis. (This example is not meant to indicate that writing itself is never reinforcing to me—it often is. However, it isn't consistently so, and much of it is clearly hard and tedious work, with the greatest reinforcement being far in the future—that is, completion of the project and its publication.)

The above paragraphs should help illustrate why I like aspects of Skinner's thinking. His ideas have practical appeal to me, and I can see that he obviously is pointing out very significant factors that control human behavior, including my own. (I have written a book that includes discussions of the impact that Skinnerian psychology has had on my life: *What Is B. F. Skinner Really Saying?*, Prentice-Hall, 1979.)

What about *Rogers*? Well, after I read his works, I generally come away feeling good. However, this is sometimes tempered by my impression that he is overly optimistic about the force toward growth and fulfillment that supposedly resides within each of us. I'm not at all sure that we will spontaneously actualize ourselves and tend toward sociable relations if we simply are accepted unconditionally by others. I lean toward Skinner's notion that achievement, cooperativeness, and other desirable behaviors must be reinforced if they are to occur regularly. Nevertheless, it can be encouraging to read Rogers' favorable comments about human nature; it's interesting to consider that, after a long career of listening to and helping troubled individuals, he strongly believes that persons are essentially rational, trustworthy, and forward-moving.

Although recently I've been most interested in the behavioral approach, Rogers' writings help keep me open and responsive to a variety of ideas, world views, and approaches to "truth." His emphasis on the necessity of different perspectives and techniques for acquiring personal and scientific knowledge seems to me to be important, though I may not agree that all approaches are equally valuable.

I'll conclude with some suggestions about a possible relationship between Rogers' and Skinner's views. Skinner, in his description of operant conditioning, gives a fairly adequate and detailed explanation of how we become what we are: through conditioning, we develop our major characteristics, including covert behaviors such as particular perceptions of ourselves and others. Assuming that this type of process takes place, Rogers' phenomenology still seems to me to be relevant; it emphasizes the importance of certain perceptions as aspects of functioning (behaving) that can be characterized as "full" or "actualized."

His suggestions for better understanding our perceptions of ourselves (self-awareness) and of others (empathy) retain their significance, not necessarily for their explanatory power but for their contribution to effective day-to-day living.

The reason for specifying "not necessarily for their explanatory power" is that I tend to agree with Skinner's assertion that the causes of our behaviors, including activities such as perceiving, are to be found ultimately in our genetic and environmental histories and in the contingencies operating in our current environment (for an intensive treatment of this topic, see Chapter 5 in Skinner's *About Behaviorism*). In other words, to say that two persons behave differently because they have different perceptions of the world is not a *final* explanation. They may have different perceptions, but the answers to both why they perceive differently *and* why their overt behaviors differ must be sought in genetic endowments and environmental conditions. Even within this Skinnerian-type context, however, it is still possible to feel, as I do, that Rogers' writings are significant; they are satisfying (reinforcing) in certain ways, and, once read, they become part of our "environmental histories," perhaps causing us to behave in more personally and socially beneficial ways.

Another potential tie between the person-centered approach and behaviorism lies in a clearer analysis of the specific behaviors involved in unconditional positive regard, empathy, and genuineness. Rogers has suggested that these so-called "attitudinal conditions" can have very beneficial effects. If they could be defined more precisely in behavioral terms (that is, what someone actually *does* when being accepting, understanding, and real), this would be useful information. It would point out certain details of interpersonal responses that possibly are positive reinforcers and might even make it easier to teach persons how to improve their interactions and relationships.

Perhaps you have a different estimate than mine of the three views of human behavior that have been discussed here, or perhaps you have found some other view to be more adequate for your purposes. Whatever the case may be, our perspectives are always limited by our particular time. The future will undoubtedly change these perspectives, but it is my opinion that the ideas of Freud, Skinner, and Rogers occupy critical niches in the progression of our thoughts about ourselves as human beings.

Index